Crunch Time

Crunch Time

How to Reengineer your Organization

James Regan

CENTURY
BUSINESS

First published 1995
© James Regan 1995
All rights reserved
James Regan has asserted his rights under the Copyright, Designs and
Patents Act, 1988, to be identified as the author of this work.

First published by
Century Ltd
Random House, 20 Vauxhall Bridge Road, London SW1V 2SA

Random House Australia (Pty) Limited
20 Alfred Street, Milsons Point, Sydney
New South Wales 2061, Australia

Random House New Zealand Limited
18 Poland Road, Glenfield
Auckland 10, New Zealand

Random House South Africa (Pty) Limited
PO Box 337, Bergvlei, South Africa

Random House UK Limited Reg. No. 954009

Papers used by Random House UK Limited are natural, recyclable
products made from wood grown in sustainable forests. The
manufacturing processes conform to the environmental regulations of
the country of origin.

ISBN 0 7126 7545 0

Contents

Preface

This book is for people whose role is to look at things from a different perspective and act. It is for those who place themselves under some pressure to perform and for the individual who defines excellence as making a difference.

The different perspective required by business today is horizontal. It's about process, interdependence and having no boundaries. You can look at something for a very long time and suddenly you see something differently. It makes you wonder. It may have been something that was staring you in the face but having seen it in new dimension you know you will never see it in the same way again. This will occur once you see an organization as a set of processes.

If you place yourself under pressure to perform, it is likely that you have the competence, insight and vision to achieve. Organizations are under a great deal of pressure to perform and to achieve. To succeed, they will need people who possess the process capability to see how things can be done differently.

People measure their success in many ways. One criterion, which seems to be accepted internationally, is how much of a difference you can make. This applies to social, political, business and family situations. Today, a difference required in organizations is to be able to alter the fundamental way to conduct business to attain a desired level of performance. Process-based activities will help make that difference.

In all of these situations there comes a point when you make the decision to move from contemplation to action. This book was written to assist you in moving from contemplating a process activity to initiating one. When you take on this responsibility to lead, it's *Crunch Time*.

Chapter One
Sum of the Parts

Current thinking about how to attain higher levels of corporate performance reflects the simple truth: the performance level of any entity or object can be attributed to how well the individual people or components function. Improving the way things work is why there exists a movement to break down organizations into processes. This is part of a natural evolution in the world of business.

A review of management literature over the past twenty years highlights the phases of this evolution. Starting with the introduction of computers and the automation of business, a natural consequence became industrial engineering and productivity improvement. This was followed by new theories on management and leadership which focused on internal organizational elements and relationships. Attention then moved externally, with companies making customer satisfaction a strategic aspect of their business initiatives. What they learned from focusing on customers was that they needed to improve quality. To achieve this they looked internally again. Now competitive pressure is requiring organizations to implement or improve processes to optimize performance. Each one of these evolutionary steps created change within organizations.

These phases comprised initiatives which occurred rapidly to fulfil business needs. If we were to investigate a corporation's history, we would probably find several remnants of these early initiatives. The way the work gets done in many companies today is often fundamentally flawed or ineffective because business processes have been constantly modified to accommodate each of these initiatives.

Another consequence of this evolution is constant modification. Current executives and managers do not fully comprehend the way their organizations operate or how and why the work gets done because they may not have been part of previous changes. Experience has shown that when asked in detail how their organization operates, many executives will admit that they simply do not have the detailed knowledge to answer properly. They indicate that it is difficult to keep up with the rate of change within their organization. More time may be spent managing changes instead of the business.

A fundamental need of managers who want to improve their organization's performance is to know how they operate. This requires an understanding of their organization's business processes.

However, obtaining this understanding is not easy. For example, a German car manufacturing executive board approved a process reengineering project. They read a number of articles and books about process-based activities and realized the importance of this latest approach. In an initial meeting to determine the scope of their proposed effort, they were asked to identify the top five processes which were critical to the success of their business plan. They could only name three. For these processes, they could not agree where they started, where they finished, who was the customer of each, nor what were the performance requirements of the processes.

The challenge facing these car manufacturing executives, was how to think and how to restructure in terms of process as opposed to layers, departments or functions.

To create a process-based organization, an executive requirement is understanding processes and their potential impact on the business. To get to the core of this understanding, the following question needs to be answered.

What are Processes?

Processes are a series of steps designed to accomplish a goal. They are three dimensional. They are linear in that they have starting and finishing points. They have width based on the number of departments involved and they have depth determined by the level of detail at which the process is documented. In addition processes have customers, beneficiaries and are driven by business, management and customer requirements. In many ways they are like building blocks. They can be created from a vision, subdivided, dismantled and re-assembled. They can also be measured, have characteristics, possess a history and are governed by a set of assumptions. Processes are the infrastructure of a company and are the primary pipeline through which corporate work flows.

What is a most interesting facet, yet most difficult to understand is how processes form this invisible grid of work flowing through a company. Many have no boundaries, some are independent and easy to manage, others are highly interdependent and complex.

Some processes are formal and represent the 'official' way of doing things. However, many of the most important processes are informal and comprise the most effective but 'unofficial' methods of working.

There are core processes and non-core processes. Some add value and others do not. Whether acknowledged or not, most processes have 'owners' but experience has often shown that ownership and accountability do not lie with the same person.

What is fascinating about examining processes is that there exist no fixed boundaries within which to define them. For example, one firm described its sales process as separate from the relationship management and resale process. Another firm described its sales process as inclusive of all these activities plus the support services.

So when embarking on a process-based activity of any type, an organization must develop both its process awareness and its process competence.

Process Awareness
This should include
- identifying the number of existing processes within an organization
- their interdependence
- the performance level of each
- the required resources to support each process
- a vision for how they should operate.

As opposed to effectively being planned, many process initiatives are guided and governed by intuition. Many companies believe that there will be positive results and significant benefits from a process activity. As often as not, significant results are achieved, but operating in this manner is like gambling with your business. A more logical way requires the executive team to rely on insight, vision, a methodology and people skilled in running process activities.

Leading by Process Competency
Successful process initiatives must be led and guided by a pre-determined set of requirements. The categories of requirements offered here are: *Business Requirements* which are the source elements, *Management Requirements* which measure operational performance and finally *Customer Requirements* which apply to product and service delivered. Example requirements for a process activity could include the following:

Business Requirements:
- time
- financial
- information technology
- people
- materials

Management Requirements:
- quality
- productivity
- volume
- cycle time
- cost

Customer Requirements:
- format
- price
- technical specifications
- delivery time

By setting targets for each of these items, the results of a process-based activity are no longer random. The extent to which these targets differ from existing performance levels will determine the amount of change needed. Once the process requirements have been reviewed and understood, then management has quantified its perspective and is ready to move forward.

Sharing Process Awareness

The next step is to share this process perspective with the organization and develop process competence. A required question to ask is whether or not you want management and employees to be literate or fluent in process-related skills. Process literacy allows managers to communicate an understanding. Fluency allows the organization to conduct process activities after the capability of individuals has been developed. Experience shows that developing fluency is the most efficient choice. To build the required level of competence it is best to use pilot process projects as a platform for learning. After each activity, training modules can be developed using examples from the organization. In this way learning is standardized, best practices documented and process competence developed within the organization.

How do Processes Impact the Business?

The Double Triangle provides a framework to answer this question. Most organizations have a vision, a mission statement, an operating set of values and a strategic plan. These four elements set the *direction* of the organization. Within these four, alignment is critical. The strategy needs to be the road map to the vision and reflect the mission of the

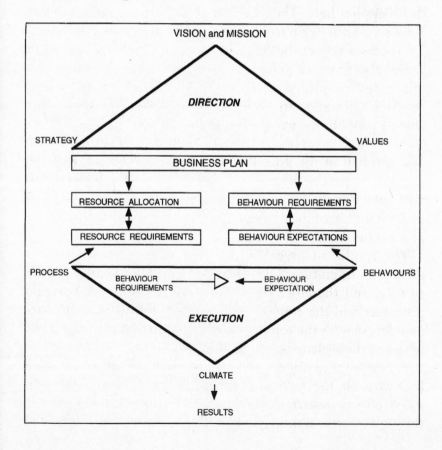

organization. In addition the values should set the tone for how the organization operates and guide how the strategy is implemented.

All of these elements come together in the annual budget or business plan. A key question should be asked of any business plan to ensure proper alignment:

> If implemented successfully does the business plan allow the organization to fulfil its strategy and vision and does it reflect the desired values?

The classic *Alice in Wonderland* quote: '. . . if you don't know where you are going, it doesn't matter how you get there' applies here. The direction of a company must be clear before you can begin to re-think and re-design its processes.

Processes reflect the established values, and any change in values also requires a change to the processes. Consistency is important for successful process activities. If a new process requires a deviation from the established values, then a major change programme may be required.

The top half of the double triangle on page 6 represents the catalyst of process changes. Execution and implementation take place and are represented in the lower half. An understanding of the dynamics at this level is important to any process initiative.

The results an organization achieves by change depends greatly on its culture. The major elements which influence the culture, and therefore the results, are the inherent business processes and the complementing skills and behaviour of its people. As with the top half of the double triangle, alignment between these elements is critical.

A key point to understand is that *processes have much more influence on the culture than behaviour.* There have been many efforts undertaken to change an organization's culture through massive training and development efforts. The results are often short-lived and disappointing because the training sets up an expectation that the new skills and behaviours are to be applied. But when people returned to the workplace, the process still required the old set of skills and behaviours. As a result, the use of the new skills declines and the climate does not fundamentally change. It is the business processes that set the skill and behavioural requirements. If the culture is to change, then processes provide the greatest leverage. How the two triangles fit and work together is the conceptual key to process initiatives.

As one executive told me at a recent workshop; 'A business plan is equivalent to a 5-ton lorry, and the processes are the beams in a bridge which must support the plan. If the bridge only has a 4-ton capacity then the plan is in predictable trouble.' Any business plan determines that year's resource allocation. But, the existing processes have their own set of resource requirements. If the allocation does not match the requirements, then the processes will need to be re-designed to require less resources. This is often not done and processes get altered randomly causing many unforeseen problems.

In a similar manner, on the people side, if the plan requires a different set of skills and behaviours, problems will occur unless a development programme is put in place. But the lead-time for behavioural change and skill acquisition is often longer than the year within which the plan is expected to be implemented. If a skill or behavioural mismatch does occur, the stress to the people is significant and the organization's capability to achieve its mission, vision, strategy and values suffers.

One organization which has undertaken the challenge to become a 'process-based' organization is Air Miles Travel Promotions Ltd, the subsidiary of British Airways which services the BA Executive Club and is the UK's largest provider of travel-based loyalty programmes. Air Miles has successfully re-structured its business to be process-based and details of their effort will be provided throughout the text.

Let's begin by examining how the Air Miles initiative started. Having completed work on the top half of the double triangle, they initiated a review of their business processes. They identified thirty-two processes which covered 95 per cent of the work. Most of these operated independently and the climate felt fragmented with behaviours being department focused with little lateral thinking, planning or communication. At a Process Review Session which occurred after the mapping of all the processes was completed, the senior management were asked to define their core business. The answer was: 'Relationship marketing and management'. They then identified their relationships. As a result, they began to re-shape the business in support of these relationships. In the final form they concluded that they had six key relationships and that they would integrate and re-design the thirty-two current processes around them. The six were:

- The Collector Management Process
- The Corporate Client Management Process
- The BA Executive Club Management Process
- The Travel Partner Management Process
- The Supplier Management Process
- The Air Miles Support Services Process

The impact of this re-configuration was significant, particularly on the management group. The departments became centres of resource and competencies which had to ensure that they could meet the requirements of the six processes. Each manager of a centre has the option of maintaining the resource internally or sourcing it externally so long as they meet the business, management and customer requirements of the processes. The role of managers changed from being leaders of a fiefdom to being members of a team serving the needs of a process.

The support infrastructure has also been altered. For example, budgets and other resources are being allocated to each of the centres, but they are based on the requirements of the process and collectively the management team works to reduce the required resource levels of each process, not their department. Much of the financial responsibility has been turned over to the centre managers. The finance role has become a service consultative one.

Reasons for Initiating a Process Activity

At the very early stages of discussions within Air Miles about becoming process-based, executives asked '*Why do we need to do this?*' After a review of what organizations typically go through to become competitive, they understood the answer and worked to avoid the mistakes of many other organizations who attempt to improve to meet the demands of the market.

In response to the requirement to improve, an organization initiates a series of activities as part of an improvement strategy. The objective at present is to reduce the level of resources required to run the business. These activities can be enacted together but they usually occur sequentially and include the following:

- budget reductions
- staff reductions
- review and elimination of non-value activities
- reducing the scope of other activities
- improving the performance of the core business activities. See diagram on page 11.

Initially, since there usually is some surplus or buffer within organizations, a reduction in resources appears to improve the performance of the company. The problem occurs when the resources are reduced below the level required to support the processes. Performance then becomes sub-optimal and can continue to decline as resources are reduced. Since

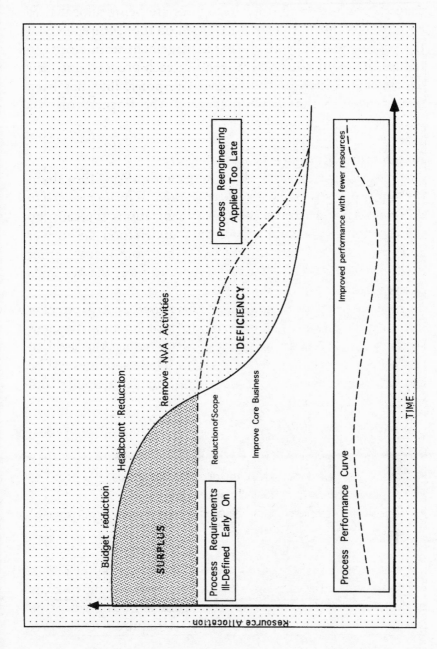

resources are allocated and reduced on a department basis, each department may stop or eliminate certain activities to

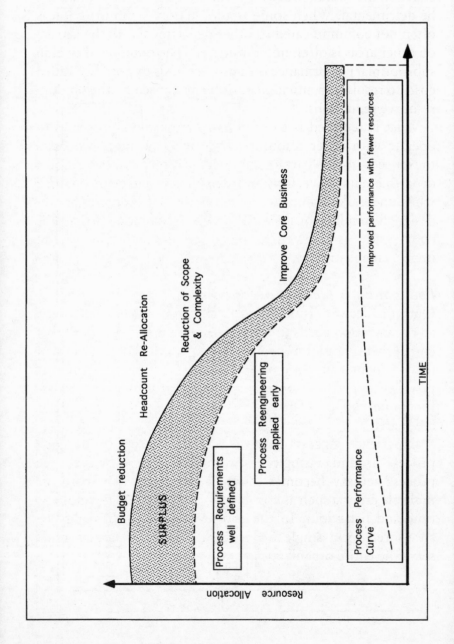

meet their resource targets. Experience has shown that as each department independently decides what it will do, the net effect on the overall processes, which are cross-functional, can be detrimental. When some step or action is eliminated, it is often not communicated to other departments, so the impact on other areas is often not considered. The outcome is overall sub-optimal performance on a process basis or possibly added costs to resolve unanticipated problems caused by the random resource reductions.

What is required is to re-design the business processes to operate with fewer resources. Improving business processes thus needs to be part of an organization's strategy, not a department initiative. Optimal performance can be maintained while undertaking improvement initiatives if processes are re-designed simultaneously with resource reduction efforts. The end result is a well-balanced implementation of an improvement strategy.

Points of Entry for Process Activities

Once the decision is made to launch a process-based activity, an organization needs to bring in *all* the stake-holders so that comprehensive requirements can be developed. It is best if management can communicate what they need from the process to perform optimally. The effort then has cross-functional support. The benefits of success as well as the risks are shared.

Experience suggests that it is relatively easy to re-design a process around a single criterion like cost. However, the process activity becomes more challenging when there are multiple criteria such as cost, quality, information technology, time and behaviour. In the end, even though they may be sponsored by a single department, process activities must serve the entire organization.

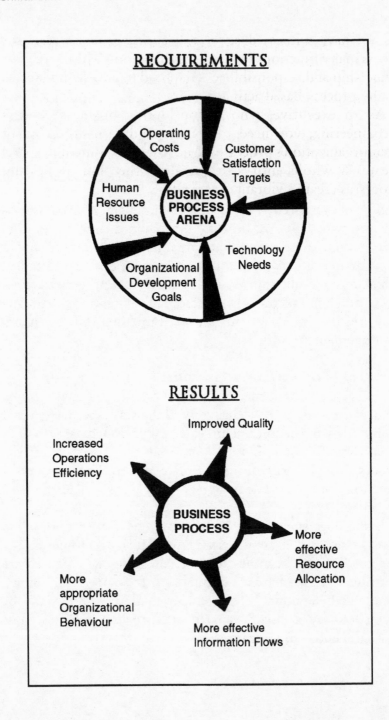

As we have witnessed again and again, processes can cut across many functions in many organizations. Therefore joint ownership and responsibility is required to ensure the success of any process-based activity.

As an executive, who is considering business process reengineering, you need to comprehend easily the core of your organization's processes. And just as the sum of the parts creates a whole entity, so too does the sum of healthy processes create a vibrant organization.

Chapter Two
The Types of Process Activities

There has been a natural evolution in the world of business to a process focus. The benefits promised by business process reengineering can read like a management wish-list. thousands of business process initiatives begin with dreams of 20 to 60 per cent improvement. The reality is often quite different.

Getting to the first step – that is comprehending your organization's processes – requires a new perspective and management consensus. A first step is to discuss what type of process-based activity is the answer to your business issue. Three types of activities are presented in this text. They are:
• Business Process Improvement
• Business Process Reengineering
• Business Process Architecture

Process questions that a management team need to answer and agree upon include:
• what is a process?
• what are an organization's key processes?
• where does a process start and finish?
• what are the business, management and customer requirements of the process?

Before making a decision to begin a process project, it pays to have the tools, materials and skills needed to ensure its ultimate success. Essentials include:

- a framework of understanding
- a methodology for conducting process activities
- a pre-determined scope of the activity
- the required resources
- an understanding of the risks
- acceptance by people involved

How many times have you begun a project at home thinking it was a relatively simple matter? It started with 'it will only take a minute' and ended up absorbing the weekend. The same could happen when your CEO asks you to champion the organization's process initiatives. Therefore, some basic pre-work is required. *This chapter is intended to highlight the prerequisites needed to make the decisions for the required process.*

The Fundamentals

As mentioned in Chapter 1, a process is a systematic series of steps designed to accomplish a goal. In its most conceptual form the entire organization is a process. But an organization is too large an entity to work with. Therefore to make process changes, the challenge is first to identify the key processes.

A process perspective is a horizontal one. It requires that you see through departmental boundaries, think laterally and recognize that processes are cross-functional.

The Systems Model

An important pre-requisite is the development of a systems perspective. To become competent in developing a systems way of thinking, occasionally reflect upon what you are doing, analyse the activity, identify the inputs needed, the process followed, the outputs achieved, and how you knew it was successful. By doing so, you are applying a systems

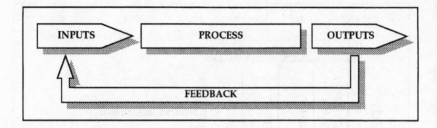

model – an activity which has inputs, process steps, outputs and a feedback loop.

For example, the next time you are sitting in a meeting try applying the systems model: you may ask what is the purpose (hence what is needed to conduct the meeting i.e. inputs), and then how the meeting is being run (i.e. process). At the end of the session you can establish the product (what the meeting accomplished i.e. outputs). Afterwards, it is straightforward to work out what you'd say to the meeting's sponsor, if he asked (i.e. feedback).

Process Change Requirements
To conduct a process activity, performance requirements need to be established. As discussed, there are three key categories. Examples of elements for which performance targets can be established are:

Business/Resources
- time
- financial
- information technology
- people
- materials

Management/Operational Requirements
- quality
- productivity
- volume
- cycle time
- cost

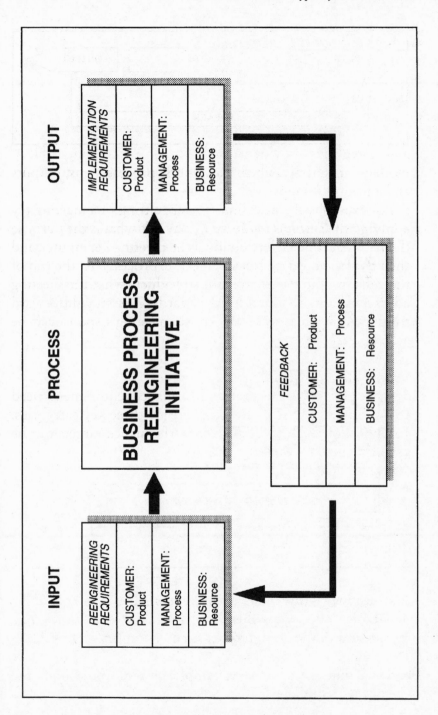

Customer/Product Requirements
- format
- price
- technical specifications
- delivery time

These categories provide a framework for communicating, measuring and tracking process performance through all stages of the systems model.

How High to Climb: The Three Levels of Process Activity

An integral part of leadership involves a vision, a mission, and a strategy. Empowering your staff, having them function as a team, and making them responsible for results, are also trademarks of a successful leader. A key leadership requirement in process activities, such as Business Process

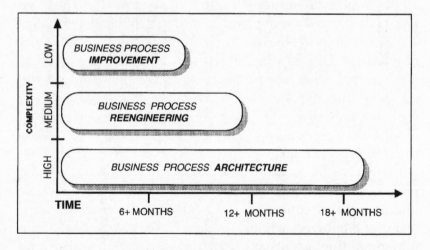

Reengineering, is the ability to make an initiative simple and manageable. Because Business Process Activities are straightforward, and are not rocket science, simplicity is possible.

Process activities vary in size, complexity and in the amount of resources required.

The most basic process activity is Business Process Improvement and the most complex is Business Process Architecture. As you increase the scope of process activity the investment, the risk and the time requirements also increase.

Level One: Business Process Improvement

Business Process Improvement is equivalent to re-decorating a house. The goal of re-decorating is to make a part of the house look and feel new. Furniture is replaced, re-upholstered and shifted. The decor, lighting and flooring are changed. However, the structure of the house, the walls and the windows, remain unchanged. This work is often do-it-yourself, sometimes with the help of the local hardware store and family members. The investment is limited, and the project is completed in a short space of time.

This type of effort in a business setting is also limited in scope, similar to re-decorating. The starting and finishing points of the process are usually within a single department. The effort supports the department's business plan and annual objectives. The results affect the performance of that department. When the project is finished, the nature of the business, and the organizational structure and boundaries, remain unchanged. The department's employees have to modify their routine and new skills are often needed to make the new process improvements work.

Improvement activities are the smallest in scope of the process activities, but not the easiest to do. It involves an initial employee education effort as the work is often done by teams of employees who, at the start of the project, have little understanding of processes or improvement tools. The employees also might not be comfortable making the decisions required to achieve significant results. They might have little experience in making decisions at work, or they might think the improvement decisions could be detrimental to their own job security. The start-up elements of the project must be handled effectively to ensure a successful effort.

This type of project is usually initiated to meet the demands of a business plan or a performance target. It might also support a corporate initiative. If a company has a quality scheme in place, it might have to examine its processes to help the scheme succeed. If the company is suffering from the financial stress of a recession, then the process effort would focus on cost factors and the elimination of waste. Improvement efforts are often one or two dimensional.

The methodology used is usually a team-based approach which is coordinated by a department manager. The team is given the project goals and a set of targets. The group builds process maps and looks at target-related elements and areas. The projects do not look at the business as a whole, only at what needs to be done to attain the desired performance requirements.

Improvement projects are a good platform for team building and teaching other types of improvement techniques such as problem solving, workplace organization, elimination of waste and root cause analysis.

This type of process project supports other continuous improvement efforts or suggestion plan systems. The key tool, a process map, is created and allows businesses to identify and act on improvement opportunities.

The business, management and customer requirements for conducting this type of process project are summarized in the diagram on page 23. The data presented is for a moderately sized project such as a customer response process or an accounts payable process.

The focus of Business Process Improvement is to enhance the existing situation. If the actions and decisions reached during the project are successfully implemented, levels of 15–25 per cent improvement can be attained. This type of activity will assist an executive to reach short-term goals but, to achieve higher levels of performance, movement to the next level of Process Activity is required.

PROCESS IMPROVEMENT

	ELEMENTS	FOCUS
BUSINESS REQUIREMENTS **AND** **RESOURCE ELEMENTS**	*Cost investment*	Under £100,000 per process
	Project time	3 - 6 months
	Assumptions	Only continuous improvement required, base process competitive
	People	Team of 10-15 people with facilitator
	Priority	Usually linked to department budget
MANAGEMENT REQUIREMENTS **AND** **OPERATIONAL ELEMENTS**	*Quality*	Problem solving used, product dimensions, incremental measurement - doing things right
	Productivity	- Team's - Unit's - Time or cost per unit
	Flexibility	Building the skills of people / Altering the workplace and department interfaces
	Relationships	Between employees
	IT	Automation of tasks / procedures Enhancements
	Cycle time	Task and Item through-put
CUSTOMER REQUIREMENTS **AND** **PRODUCT ELEMENTS**	*Format*	Set by receiving unit
	Delivery time	Meets hourly / weekly time frames
	Price	Not calculated
	Functional aspect	- Useability - Accessibility - Reliability
	Technical specification	Completeness

Level Two: Business Process Reengineering

The domestic equivalent to *Business Process Reengineering* is re-modelling a house. It requires you to knock down walls, replace windows and change the boundaries within the house. Because of the structural changes, the house feels and looks dramatically different. To re-model, you form and coordinate a team of craftsmen and designers.

Those involved must have a clear set of requirements, blueprints and a vision of the re-designed house. The investment is considerable and often takes months to complete.

Reengineering results in companies being re-modelled. Projects can be expansive in scope. The starting point and finishing point of a targeted process are usually in different departments, making it cross-functional. Areas involved are those which have an impact on, or are impacted by, the process being reengineered.

A reengineering effort supports the company's business plan. The focus is to achieve benefits in support of mid-term targets which are three to four years in the future. The results of a successful project contribute to corporate performance and should be tracked to the bottom line within a year of implementation.

A typical project can take up to six months. The implementation of the decisions required to complete the project can take another one to two years. When finished, the fundamental business remains the same but the organizational structure, traditional boundaries, rules and responsibilities are drastically altered. The organization has a new routine of improvement.

New skills are needed to make the reengineered processes work. As in the case of the previously mentioned Business Process Improvement projects, it is the people who can make or break the effort.

The competence requirements of people working in a reengineered process must be identified and employees trained. This is particularly true for management. After a process is reengineered, decisions are likely be made at lower levels, and the level of authority and responsibility of line workers is increased. The managers' and supervisors' roles change dramatically. They have to learn to manage process and the competence needed, with less focus on their traditional role.

Although employees provide much of the information needed in a reengineering project, it is management who have the greatest influence. They must review the assumptions behind the process as well as set the performance requirements. Management development is needed before, during and after a project to ensure a working understanding of the concepts, tools, requirements and consequences.

Tradition is the greatest challenge to success. Managers tend to protect their departments which leads them to seeing and understanding only part of the overall business. Business Process Reengineering projects cross departmental lines and support multiple strategic initiatives. Therefore managers need to see the business as a whole and make the required decisions to reach the targeted performance levels. If affected managers do not see how a Reengineering project can improve the company as a whole, they might view it as a disruption to their department's normal activities and block the process during implementation.

To overcome management adherence to the status quo, a full set of business, management and customer requirements must be established at a very early stage. Setting the requirements becomes a platform for management involvement and the sharing of views. Another way to unfreeze traditional views is to identify the underlying assumptions of the targeted process and ask why it operates the way it does. The assumptions need to be validated, altered or suspended. Discussing and changing the assumptions of the business helps develop a consensus on management's views . . . It also creates a freedom of thought for building a new process. Identifying requirements and assumptions are key concepts underlying the methodology for conducting Business Process Reengineering projects.

Visualizing the process is another key to success. In every process project, it is the process map which makes clear both the obstacles and the opportunities. People are often surprised when they see a process map. It gives them a new, accurate and incisive view of the process not seen before. The Reengineering project usually gets all the support it needs after a process map is built and properly communicated, because it allows the people involved to see the issues and support the needed change.

The business, management and customer requirements of a moderately sized Business Process Reengineering project are summarized in the next chart and would apply to examples such as a product development process, a corporate planning process or many of the large financial and product based processes in a company.

The focus of Business Process Reengineering is to radically alter the way the company operates. Our experience in, for example, the automobile manufacturing industry suggests that the effective implementation of actions and decisions reached during a reengineering project can lead to 25–45 per cent improvement in the business. This type of activity helps an executive team reach medium-term goals based on the market and competition. If reengineering the large strategic processes is not enough to meet performance requirements, movement to the final level of Process Activity must be considered.

Level Three: Business Process Architecture

When the infrastructure of a house cannot provide the support required, and improvement efforts reflect the law of diminishing returns, then it is time to consider a total overhaul. *Business Process Architecture* is the equivalent activity for a company. It is comparable to gutting an old

PROCESS REENGINEERING

	ELEMENTS	FOCUS
BUSINESS REQUIREMENTS **AND** **RESOURCE ELEMENTS**	*Cost investment*	£100,000 - £500,000
	Project time	12 months or more
	Assumptions	There exists a major interface / business / cross functional issue
	People	Technical team of 3 - 5 with standing management support group
	Priority	Linked to business plan
MANAGEMENT REQUIREMENTS **AND** **OPERATIONAL ELEMENTS**	*Quality*	Problem prevention, Process quality, doing the right thing
	Productivity	- Departments - Budget - Item / time or cost
	Flexibility	Boundaries / methodologies
	Relationships	Between functions
	IT	Integrate functions / info New system installation
	Cycle time	Cross-functional operations
CUSTOMER REQUIREMENTS **AND** **PRODUCT ELEMENTS**	*Format*	Set by overall corporate requirements
	Delivery time	Meets planning requirements
	Price	To Budget / plan
	Functional aspect	Repeatable / dependable
	Technical specification	Best Practice

building or constructing a new one. You start with a clean sheet of paper, with the objective being to achieve an overall change. Experts are needed, the investment and the risks are substantial, the project can take years to complete and there are no guarantees of achieving the desired returns. The rearchitecting of General Electric is frequently cited in the literature as one of the classic examples of a successful, complete overhaul of a large corporation.

This type of effort is unlimited in scope. The focus is on the entire business. You start the project by questioning the existing marketplace assumptions, the corporate strategy and the business itself. The finishing point could be a decision to lead your industry in innovation and work in a completely new way. Much of the information needed to make decisions in a project of this type comes from research and technology. Benchmarking is often an early step. An Architecture effort is a platform for innovation because there are few restrictions in determining what could be possible.

To architect initiatives will incur major investment, involve board-level approvals and mean that returns are calculated on a long-term basis. Effective Business Process Architecture heavily involves information technology. Modelling and simulation are helpful tools to determine what is possible and to assess the risk involved.

When the project is completed the organization will have an entirely new structure with radically different operating guidelines. The company will need to change its view on the way it works.

Process Architecture projects also result in major corporate culture change. New processes at the corporate level set new technical and behavioural requirements for the entire organization. The combined effect of these two elements on the culture of the company is dramatic and makes the implementation stage synonymous with an effort to change the culture within an organization. You are not just changing the process when the work is of this magnitude . . . you are

PROCESS ARCHITECTURE

	ELEMENTS	FOCUS
BUSINESS REQUIREMENTS **AND** **RESOURCE ELEMENTS**	*Cost investment*	£500,000 plus
	Project time	1 - 4 years
	Assumptions	Major parts of the business are not competitive
	People	Team of experts, management committee and task teams
	Priority	Linked to strategic plan
MANAGEMENT REQUIREMENTS **AND** **OPERATIONAL ELEMENTS**	*Quality*	Market / Perceived image/ Customer satisfaction
	Productivity	Corporate basis
	Flexibility	Structural and strategic
	Relationships	Competition Shareholders
	IT	Total integration of IT
	Cycle time	Strategic response/ Organisational Learning
CUSTOMER REQUIREMENTS **AND** **PRODUCT ELEMENTS**	*Format*	Set by market requirements
	Delivery time	Meets strategic objectives
	Price	To customer To profit plan / forecast
	Functional aspect	Reliability for future applications
	Technical specification	World class

changing an organization. Major investment will be needed for training at all levels, particularly for executives who are essential to the project's success.

The challenge of an architecture project is to have both the experts and the executive team think outside the normal boundaries and not be restrained by previous experiences. A project takes what is possible, or impossible, and makes it a reality. Results are limited only by the creativity of the participants working on the project.

The business, management and customer requirements of a Business Process Architecture project are summarized in the diagram on page 29, where the data is for a moderately sized project.

The focus of Business Process Architecture is to create a new business environment and gain a distinct competitive advantage. Improvements can reach 40–65 per cent with the effective implementation of the actions and decisions reached during the effort.

Architecture will assist an executive team achieve its long-term goals. If re-building large corporate processes does not attain the needed levels of performance, it could be time to consider drastic measures to obtain assistance. A merger or strategic alliance are possible alternatives.

Communication: Keep it Clear and Simple
Communication of a process initiative to the company is crucial. Unfortunately, the language of the initiative is often laden with jargon. By being familiar with the jargon, it is possible to become aware of the potential for confusion, and define the terms your organization will use. Here is a tool to select a name for your communication process. Take any one word from the following:

core	strategic
business	corporate
continuous	cross-functional
global	tactical

Place the word 'process' after it, and then add any one word from the following:

improvement	engineering
design	re-design
modelling	re-modelling
reengineering	architecture

As long as you consistently use your terminology, and keep the vocabulary simple, you will have eliminated an early problem.

To be clear and concise, the focus of the effort has to be determined. If the focus is on the business, then we are reengineering the business, if the focus is on the process, then we are reengineering the process. The word 'reengineering' has filtered into many diverse areas outside the business community with professionals offering to reengineer personal lives and relationships. Hence, there is the need to maintain a standard vocabulary and be consistent in communication.

Currency of Improvement
In its simplest form, a process-based activity is nothing more than a tool to help make decisions. The three types of process activities described are like different size hammers. You must select the right tool for the job. There is no need for a sledge hammer to hang a picture.

Process initiatives are focused activities concentrating on 'how' the work gets done. It is important to remember that processes are only one dimension of a business, albeit a critical one. Improving, reengineering or building new processes will streamline and improve your business, but the initiatives will not take into account how best to analyse and tackle a market or take advantage of competitors' weaknesses.

Process activities are tangible steps to a goal, and they cannot work without people. Too many process initiatives focus only on the business dimensions. Everyone has heard a story about the office which had computers installed on all the desks and today most remained unused. The same scenario can happen with processes. You could install a new process in the business but people continue to work in the old manner. Processes, like computers, are only as good as the people behind them. People and processes must mesh so that the desired level of improvements can be achieved.

Decisions are the commodities of process improvement, reengineering and architecture initiatives. It is decision-making competence, above most other skills, that will make process activities a success. Possessing this competence will allow executives to navigate their way readily through the challenging waters of process.

Chapter Three
Strategic Overview

A point of view in this book is that *Decisions are the commodity of process-based activities.* The alternative view could be that a new process is the outcome of a process activity. A new process map is a dream which requires a set of decisions to be implemented to make it a reality. The common denominator for all process activities is that they are decision-making platforms. The initial setting-up, the process mapping, data analyses, and the measuring of performance represent the information needed to make decisions. Once the decisions are made, the activity shifts to project management, where implementation of the decisions and subsequent tracking is the focal point.

You end up with a high performing process if and when the decisions to alter a process are implemented and monitored successfully.

Any approach, including the one presented here, represents a point of view on how to obtain information, how to make decisions and how to get them implemented. You will find little difference between the basic methods which are readily available in the marketplace. However, you will find significant differences in the assumptions behind an approach, what type of end product is promised, and the tools used and the method by which process improvements are implemented and measured.

Before any approach is actually applied, it is critical to understand the current business need, the past and the future requirements. For a consulting firm, the business situation is often summarized in a tender document and proposals are reviewed by an organization to determine the 'fit' of an approach.

Examining an actual tender involving one of the largest European airlines will serve to illustrate the thinking behind it and steps required before actually initiating a process project.

The text of a tender follows.

IMPROVEMENT OF MANAGEMENT PROCESSES

Background

The firm had just completed a review of overheads and concluded that:

- Depending on definition, between 16 per cent and 35 per cent of the staff are employed in overhead activity. 12 per cent of all staff are employed in central and support departments.
- Management numbers have grown much faster than total staff numbers over the last ten years. Recent growth has occurred mainly in support departments. Despite a lean structure at the top of the organization, the central and support management structures generally are tall and narrow.
- Seven cross-functional processes are the major causes of concern and require attention. These are:
  - Human Resource Planning
  - Budget Setting
  - Financial Approval (including cross-functional approval)
  - Business Planning
  - Internal Financial Reporting
  - Business Reporting
  - Internal Financial Charging

Some of the above processes (e.g. Business Planning & Financial Approvals) had already been reviewed by an internal investigative team. This revealed that four fundamental problem issues had been identified that underlie many of them:

- Lack of clear business priorities
- Unclear accountability and responsibility
- Ineffective decision-making processes
- Excessive centralist controls

As a result of the review, the firm had decided to reduce management layers, increase the number of direct reports per manager, and make a significant reduction in the number of management grade staff.

Management numbers are being reduced through early retirement and voluntary severance with a target saving of 10 per cent. This has provided a significant impetus for improvement of the management processes.

The firm now wishes to improve management effectiveness as well as realize further cost savings by improving cross-functional processes by addressing the issues that lie behind them.

Overall Process Activity Objectives
The primary objectives for this project are as follows:
- To achieve better, more effective decision-making (i.e. quicker, more effective and more market responsive)
- To achieve further sustainable reductions in overhead costs
- To give line managers a greater sense of responsibility and authority to match their accountabilities
- To support the current reduction in management numbers

Secondary but also important objectives are:
- To achieve early improvements
- To increase the level of skills in Process Improvement and Project Management with the firm

These goals are to be achieved by:
- the simplification of controls and moving decisions closer to the line
- the simplification and reduction of the workload and bureaucracy involved in the seven cross-functional processes
- possible out-sourcing of some services currently carried out within support departments

The firm recognizes that this is potentially a very large project, and that a phased approach will be necessary. Specific objectives for Phase 1 are therefore:

- To identify and develop the following:
  - the current role, cost and effectiveness of each of the seven processes (listed on the first page of this tender)
  - the optimal balance between line responsibility, required central control and simplified procedures
  - and out-sourcing policy for activities in support departments
- To create a vision for improvement of the seven cross-functional processes and develop plans for the migration to that vision
- To identify major changes to managerial and staff roles, skills and competencies
- To develop a high level approach to managing the resulting change and its impact on managers and staff
- To improve internal project management and process improvement skills
- To develop appropriate leadership roles to take the project forward
- To achieve some early process improvements

Whilst the scope of this project is broad, covering the whole of the core airline company, major change to current organizational or reporting structures is to be avoided. The present structure (with some minor changes) appears to provide the 'right' economic levers to produce performance. Also a commitment has been given that no unnecessary major change will be made quickly. However, out-sourcing of services carried out within support departments can be considered.

Detailed below is the current view of the required approach.

It is anticipated that the first phase will be undertaken through work at two levels in the organization which together should meet the Objectives and Deliverables specified in this brief:

- at the senior executive level, the work will be undertaken through facilitated discussions with senior executives. These discussions will resolve key project issues and allow the firm's overall strategic direction to drive the process.
- at the working level, process analysis work will be undertaken in at least three areas of the business (e.g. a passenger terminal, a production unit such as catering, and an overseas area), in order to identify the interaction between the seven cross-functional processes and the core business processes.

The results of this process work will be expected to provide an arena for validation of the conclusions of the senior executive work. There should also be tangible results from the work in these areas of the business in terms of process improvement opportunities. Based on the success of the approach, the process will be rolled out to other areas in later phases.

Considerations
Existing initiatives and frameworks must be considered when developing the way forward.

Deliverables
The primary deliverables from this phase are:
- key *policy decisions* that are required before effective progress can be made
- a convincing *case for action* that can be communicated within the organization
- a *vision* for the changed processes
- a *business case* predicted on the changed processes
- a *migration plan,* including integration with existing initiatives and policies for managing changes to staff numbers and roles
- *early improvements* providing tangible benefits in the selected areas of the business to prove the initiative

- *transfer of skills* in process improvement and project management

Project Milestones & Time Scales
Within the first phase of this project, the vision and early recommendations will be provided to all directors within eight weeks.

Phase 1 Final Review which will include:
- agreed case for action
- agreed vision of the changed processes
- agreed business case
- agreed migration plan
- management process improvement in the selected areas of the business

A summary of the seven processes to be reviewed:

Manpower Planning Controls and Information
There is currently a lack of clarity regarding policy and overall strategy for manpower planning and development. Resource planning activity seems uncoordinated, with corporate activities in Human Resources being duplicated in line departments. Despite the Business Plan and Budget processes, all external recruitment is scrutinized by a third input control mechanism, the Human Resource Management Committee.

Training and personal administration policies are confused and disparate, resulting in high levels of duplicated effort and diluted value for money.

Budget Process
The budget process is seen as cumbersome and resource intensive for all participants: it also appears to have little direct correlation to either the Business Plan or the overall Corporate objectives. It is regarded as a very lengthy process

which concentrates effort and focus on input control rather than analysis and use of information for business improvement. The frequent changes to targets during the build up also cause concern. Such uncertainty over the long time scales involved clearly impedes flexibility and the capability to react to changing circumstances.

Financial Approvals

The approvals process for capital items and major service projects (e.g. advertising campaigns) is divorced from the Business Plan and Budget processes and places heavy emphasis on input challenge of proposals and claimed benefits. It is seen as a lengthy and resource intensive process even for relatively small value items, with the added scrutiny of a separate approval process for high cost items. This creates the perception that responsibility and accountability are removed from the line department by both the number and relative seniority of the approvals required for each project.

While the Approvals process undoubtedly weeds out some ill-conceived or low return projects, the fact that no consistent method for post audit of project benefits exists, makes it difficult to conclude one way or the other whether the existing method is most appropriate to business benefit.

Financial Reporting

The main issues concerned with financial reporting are around the overlap between the finance department and line activities, particularly parallel activities between Corporate Finance, Line Finance and departmental business managers. One outcome of this is the multiplicity of reports and inconsistency of data. Efforts have been made by Finance to focus reporting but the cross-functional issues indicate that there is still concern over the time and effort that financial reporting demands. In addition, there would appear to be more effort going into the process of producing the reports than the analysis.

Business Reporting

Business reporting shares many of the issues raised under financial reporting. However, here the overlap exists between line departments as well as between central and line departments. Again this leads to a multiplicity of reports and inconsistency of data. The problem of data inconsistency is not helped by the lack of a single source.

This leads to effort spent on reconciling different views of business performance and validating numbers. Several departments raised issues over the unavailability, unreliability and inconsistency of data. Overall, this seems to result in effort being focused more on input, i.e. the impact on the business.

Business Planning Process

Several issues pointed to a lack of coordination in business planning. This manifests itself in a tension between commercial flexibility and operational certainty. Poor specification to the delivery departments then leads to poor performance. There would appear to be no method for timely conflict resolution or responsibility and accountability to be determined and understood.

Internal Recharge Process

The internal recharge process is a complex and highly resource intensive method of distributing central facilities costs across the business. It is seen as a cumbersome mechanism which enhances centralized decision-making, rather than empowering managers in the line. In some cases, cross charges can comprise over 50 per cent of the budget, yet the line manager's ability to influence or reduce these costs in the short to medium term is very limited. This creates a contradictory perception of 'service' functions appearing to act as control mechanisms which add significant cost but little value to the customer.

[End of tender]

The Tender Response

A simple framework for determining what needed to be done is a learning model that came from Stanford University. It states that there are three basic stages you must go through before finally taking action. They are becoming aware,

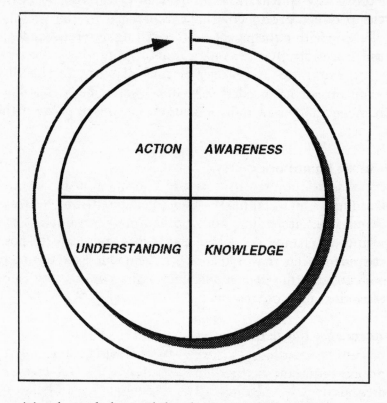

acquiring knowledge and developing understanding.

The tender document communicated their awareness of their business situation. However, they did not have the required knowledge nor the level of understanding needed to proceed or take action. The following categories are areas that this organization needed to have knowledge about:

- Common issues – in this case, were there similar problems underlying all seven processes?

- Prioritize processes – which of these processes had the greatest strategic importance and contributed the most 'value-added' to the organization?

- Process assessment/analysis – a review of the complexity of the product produced, the competence of the people working within the process and the overall performance of the process itself

- Type of activity needed – does it require improvement, reengineering or an architecture type project?

- Structure of the project – determining the scope, the logic and the framework

- Readiness – determining if the organization is ready for a process-based project by assessing the organization's history of change, ownership of the initiative, the level of support within the organization, the project's alignment with the overall strategy and other initiatives and the level of clarity of the expected results

- The plan – the actual project plan based on the particular process methodology selected and identifying what the project requirements are and the sources of the resources needed

- Risks – A quality gate in which a risk assessment of the entire project is conducted to increase the likelihood of success. A major area of risk is where the stress on the organization is the greatest. So it is important to identify and be sensitive to where in the organization the project is likely to have the greatest impact and to develop a support plan

Working through the above elements provided the knowledge and understanding required to approve a process project. It is in the set-up and preparation that most of the future problems are created, or prevented, therefore it is critical that, to avoid the effort from becoming another executive experiment or the 'effort du jour', a disciplined working through of the learning wheel be executed. It sets the tone for the effort if the executive team models this discipline and it makes the entire effort more credible.

All of the above elements were incorporated into the development of the proposal in addition to the elements required by the tender. A review of each of them in more detail and how they were applied to this request will provide the required level of knowledge and understanding to set up a process project. Later we will go into detail about how a process-based activity could be conducted.

Size of the Process
This is the critical consideration as it affects every aspect of the process initiative. It influences the project resource requirement, the competence level of those involved as the issues are more complex. It also affects the timing, the level of support needed and the risks. The larger the process, the more eggs that are being placed in the same basket.

In this situation, the organization could have considered planning as a single process. If so, HR and Business Planning would have been part of the same process as well as the budget. In a process-based company, all three entities would probably be integrated under one process umbrella. However, in this case, the choice was made to segment them, which reflected the departmental influence of the organization and their desire to achieve early results.

Common Issues
A review of summaries of the seven processes provided in the tender yielded several similar types of problems. They were:

- duplication
- coordination
- insufficient input requirements
- lack of standard practices
- few output measures
- time management and cycle time
- level of resources required or applied
- lack of accountability
- quality and usability of data from the processes

If these were common to all seven processes listed at the start of this tender, then they are indicators of corporate-wide problems. It raises the issue of whether or not these problems should be addressed on a corporate-wide rather than on an individual process-by-process basis. Some of them indicate a cultural issue (accountability), some are training based (time issues), and others indicate an overall deficiency in management practices. This insight reveals indicators of the corporate culture. These are an early warning system of resistance and problems that could occur within the project and during the implementation stages.

Prioritize Processes
Given the objectives and the performance requirements of a process project, criteria are needed to determine the importance of each process. The criteria often vary and depend on the term of the outlook of the executive team. If the outlook is short-term, then a quick return on investment often becomes the number one criterion. However, if the perspective is long-term, then the threshold is likely to be linked to how the project can contribute to the strategy.

There is also the common sense element that often takes precedence over any business criteria. For example in this project, given that the tender appeared a little before the start of their planning cycle, those processes that were annual and linked to the corporate calendar went to the forefront. The reason being that there was a window for improving the processes and have them work in the next cycle while waiting meant that the opportunity to implement would have to wait a year.

There are criteria to help prioritize process activities:
- which are most closely linked to or represent the core business?
- which offer the most potential value-added if improved?
- in what order do the processes flow in the natural sequence of the business?
- which processes are in most dire need of repair or are least competitive?
- which are the most complex and will take the longest time to attain a result?

It is challenging to conduct process-based activities on many processes simultaneously. Even at the macro level, there is a degree of interdependence between the processes and it is likely that changes in one process may impact another. Therefore, there should be a process sequence in the project based on the prioritization. For example, in this airline case, if a new budgetary process eliminated the need for cross charging, why invest a great deal in changing the internal charging process at the same time?

Process Assessment and Analysis

Once the scope of each process has been determined and its priority assigned, the next step to keep the process-based activity on track and focused is an assessment. In many ways it is equivalent to either an estimator doing an auto damage report or a doctor conducting a physical. In either case they determine what needs to be done based on what they learn.

For a process assessment, the 'doctors' are the managers who work within the process. They take a look at the operation. The assessment examines the business, the competence of the people and the performance of the process

Process Assessment Framework

Business Assessment	Competence Assessment	Process Assessment
Complexity	Skill of Team	Lead-time Estimate
Innovation	Experience of Team	Resource Allocation
Scope	History of Change	Cost
Sensitivity		Risk
Technology		Quality
		Structure

Global Assessment

NEW REQUIREMENTS: **Rating**

Change in Content	Change / Develop People	Re-set Parameters and make Process Changes

itself. The result is a rating. This rating indicates the type and the scope of activity most appropriate to meet the business criteria.

The assessment may indicate that the process cannot adequately support the business or the product it produces. If so, a decision is required to either rapidly repair the process, alter the product in line with the capability of the organization or, make an investment in developing people. The assessment tool will be presented in detail in Chapter 5. The other major benefit of the assessment is that it will highlight what needs to be improved within the organization *prior* to starting. If the assessment finds that the organization does not have a common problem-solving or decision-making tool in place, then how will people make consistent decisions or resolve problems? Or if there is a lack of knowledge about quality, you cannot assume that a team improving a process will insert the steps required to prevent problems or ensure first time quality. A diagnosis of the people, the process and the product produced is needed to ensure that the requirements of the process identified are met.

Type of Activity Needed

As discussed in Chapter 2, all processes do not require a major effort to get them to perform to the desired level. The results of the assessment provide the information needed to make this decision. A root course analysis of the issues diagnosed in the assessment will allow the identification of the requirements needed to resolve them. If the performance levels can be reached through minor modifications or major changes to only small parts of the process, then the scope of the effort could be limited to a process improvement effort. If the problems are widespread and are of a cross-functional nature, it is likely that a reengineering project is required. And if the process is fundamentally flawed throughout then an architecture type project would be required. Every process has its own type of solution and all projects do not need major initiatives. An assessment was completed on each of the seven processes.

Structure of the Project

This is equivalent to the development of the master plan. The responsible person or team needs to determine the activity sequence. The organization has a limit for the amount of change it can handle and the level of resource which will be applied. A review of the impact on individual departments is also required. If, for example, all of the process initiatives require the involvement of the finance department, can that department fulfil its role in the process initiatives and continue the running of the business at the same time? It is easy to overload a particular department in the development of the structure; the overall impact of the master plan has to be determined at the corporate and departmental levels and, if necessary, at the individual level.

In this case, four processes were clustered and tagged

PROCESS	TYPE OF ACTIVITY	APPROACH
'A' Priority: Linked to Corporate Calendar		
• Human Resource Planning and Data Processes • Budgetary Processes • Business Planning Process • Internal Charging Process	• Reengineering • Architecture • Improvement • Reengineering	- Consultant-led - Business Platform - Complete before next Business Cycle - Accelerated effort
'B' Priority: Open timing		
• Financial Approvals Process • Internal Financial Reporting Process • Business Reporting Process	• Improvement • Improvement • Improvement	- Joint Client/Consultant Project - Learning platform - Completed before 'Full Implementation of Pilot' - Follows 'A' Priority items by 2 months

	COMMON ISSUES	
DUPLICATION	COORDINATION	ACCURACY
INPUT REQUIREMENTS	STANDARD PRACTICES	OUTPUT MEASURES
TIME	LEVEL OF RESOURCE	ACCOUNTABILITY

priority A where the process initiative would be focused with time deadlines. Three other processes were rated priority B and would be used as a learning platform with an open schedule which followed the A activities by least two months.

Readiness
Once the overall project structure is complete it is a good idea to test the readiness of the organization to determine any major obstacles to the effort. There are five categories:

History of change which looks at the organization's track

record in implementing major initiatives. You can learn a great deal from a corporation's history of change and in this case you may be able to identify any additional steps which will prevent previous problems recurring or determine what was successful to see if these practices can be included in this project.

Clarity around the expected results which ensures that the organization understands and has the same expectations of what the project will yield. Often the moon is promised, but this element acts as a reality check. When you communicate the desired results and the management team expresses disbelief and gives you ten reasons why, you can then identify additional barriers to the desired level of performance and take the appropriate action.

Ownership of the initiative is a less tangible but just as critical element. Within the organization, efforts like process activities usually start out as the idea of an executive. If the source has a poor reputation for any reason or if an executive group indicates their support for 'their' initiative, you get a sense of the future level of commitment and level of accountability for the results. Prior to starting, the ownership has to be expanded to a wider audience and not attributed to one person. A final consideration is that if the person who starts the initiative appears to be the one least affected, then the effort will not have a balanced sense of commitment. It could be seen as an intervention from the outside which in turn would generate significant resistance to implementation.

The plan is ready to be prepared once the above items are successfully dealt with. At this stage, the actual activities are scheduled and timing is attached to the structure, resources are budgeted and critical path and other project management tools (e.g. quality gates) are incorporated within the project.
At this stage, it becomes vital to assign roles and

responsibilities. Therefore the corporate commitment to change is directly influenced and the performance requirements of the project determined. The plan has to be credible and realistic. What has been learned from completing the other work needs to be reflected in the plan. If the organization feels the plan is achievable when it is communicated, people will be less hesitant to start. If the plan is too aggressive, resistance at the working level will probably be the outcome, as it will be perceived that the disruption to the operation does not match the benefits. The importance of how the plan is communicated cannot be overlooked. Many potentially beneficial initiatives trip over this first step. The key elements in the communication are honesty: what is

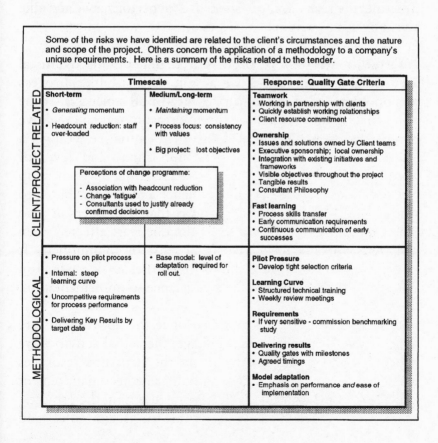

Some of the risks we have identified are related to the client's circumstances and the nature and scope of the project. Others concern the application of a methodology to a company's unique requirements. Here is a summary of the risks related to the tender.

	Timescale		Response: Quality Gate Criteria
	Short-term	**Medium/Long-term**	**Teamwork** • Working in partnership with clients • Quickly establish working relationships • Client resource commitment
CLIENT/PROJECT RELATED	• *Generating* momentum • Headcount reduction: staff over-loaded	• *Maintaining* momentum • Process focus: consistency with values • Big project: lost objectives	**Ownership** • Issues and solutions owned by Client teams • Executive sponsorship; local ownership • Integration with existing initiatives and frameworks • Visible objectives throughout the project • Tangible results • Consultant Philosophy
	Perceptions of change programme: - Association with headcount reduction - Change 'fatigue' - Consultants used to justify already confirmed decisions		**Fast learning** • Process skills transfer • Early communication requirements • Continuous communication of early successes
METHODOLOGICAL	• Pressure on pilot process • Internal: steep learning curve • Uncompetitive requirements for process performance • Delivering Key Results by target date	• Base model: level of adaptation required for roll out.	**Pilot Pressure** • Develop tight selection criteria **Learning Curve** • Structured technical training • Weekly review meetings **Requirements** • If very sensitive - commission benchmarking study **Delivering results** • Quality gates with milestones • Agreed timings **Model adaptation** • Emphasis on performance *and* ease of implementation

required, and how will those requirements affect them, both positively and negatively?

Determining the risks is an ongoing activity based on the performance of the project. Every project has the potential to derail. At the start and at key points in the project, risks have to be determined and reviewed. It should be an inherent element of running process activities. There are a number of risk assessment methods and one should be incorporated into the project. These methods allow risk to be categorized by type and, over time, can be assessed with contingency responses in place if the risk gets too great.

After the activities described above have been completed, the project is ready to be launched. The organization should have the necessary knowledge and understanding to complete the initiative with an excellent chance of success.

With this overview of process activities and the required decisions to support them, we now look step by step at the methodology for conducting a process-based activity.

Chapter Four Methodology Summary and Phase 1: Initiate the Project

There are three major segments or stages in any process activity:
- Collect and provide the *information* needed to make decisions
- Make the *decisions*
- Develop project plan and *implement* the decisions

The first three chapters have focused on how to decide what needs to be done. The remainder of the book will focus on the actual methods and tools needed to conduct process-based activities. Depending on one's preference, there could be any number of phases to conduct these activities. However, the actual methodology in this text has five phases and is applicable to all three types of process activities – Improvement, Reengineering and Architecture (as discussed in Chapter 2). It is important to understand the steps and the exit criteria which have been formatted into these five phases.

In this methodology, the first three phases describe the information collection related activities and the last two deal with decision-making and implementation.

As defined earlier, this approach is based on the position

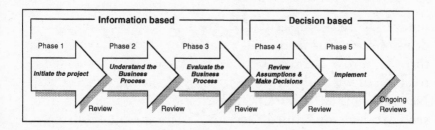

that the real commodities of any process activity will be the decisions.

Despite the recent fanfare and claims to greatness, *process reengineering, re-design, modelling, or any other name it is given, is a decision-making tool to tackle complex business process problems.*

This perspective is important to adopt. Even though the word 'process' is dominant in the materials you come across, the name of the game is 'decisions'. When you approach it from this simpler viewpoint your understanding of process activities and methodologies can be greatly enhanced.

Take juggling as an example of taking a different perspective and being successful. Juggling is something that many people do and many others want to do. Even though a juggler makes it appear easy, many people become all thumbs when asked to try. They understand what is supposed to happen but find it difficult to transfer what they know and see into action. Just as decisions are the secret to process activity there is a similar secret to juggling.

The secret in juggling is *throwing.*

Simple. When people try to juggle and toss the first ball they immediately become pre-occupied with *catching* the first ball and they forget to toss the second. Their anxiety about catching prohibits their release of the other balls.

The pre-occupation with catching is what prevents people from learning to juggle: just as being too focused on process and not on decisions will prevent an organization from fully completing a process activity. The secret of juggling is to think *throw.* You are not juggling if that second and third ball do not get tossed. Similarly, you are not reengineering if the decisions are not made and implemented. So if you think: throw 1, throw 2, throw 3, throw 1, throw 2 … The ball tends to come down without the assistance of the juggler. Sir Isaac Newton figured that out. In business think first decision, second decision, third decision. The result will be a reengineering process.

Our initial step is to look at the methodology phase by phase. The structure of each phase will be presented as follows:

- Summarize the **Purpose** of each phase
- Identify the **Products**
- Document the **Process** of each phase
- List the **Exit Criteria** for the phase
- Review the **Tools and Methods** used in the phase
- Highlight **Risks** and how to prevent problems

Sample material and case examples will be used to reinforce key concepts.

Phase 1–Initiate the Project

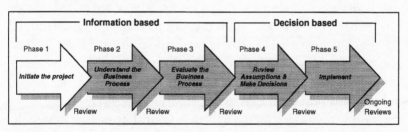

The **purpose** of this phase is to collect and communicate the information required to ensure an effective and *efficient start-up* of the process activity.

The **product** is *commitment* of people and resource to move forward.

The **process** within this phase has three elements: *Education, Structure* and *The Project Contract.*

Education

The activities within this element are driven by three needs which must be met: 1. The *organization* needs to know about the process initiative; 2. *Management* needs to have knowledge about process concepts and the methodology; and 3. If there is a desire to have an internal process capability, a *technical training programme* on process tools and methods is required.

1. The *organization*'s need for information about the initiative can be met by providing and communicating:
   - *Assumptions* behind the initiative
   - Business *need* for the initiative with supporting data
   - Project *goals* and how they support the strategy and business plan
   - Project *requirements* in terms of time and expected results
   - *Names* of the processes selected
   - Type of *activity* to be used on each process
   - Perceived *risks* and how the project will impact the organization
   - Confirmation of the organization's *readiness*
   - Project *leadership*

   This information can be delivered through an existing communication channel such as a newsletter or, if a package is developed, it can be cascaded through the organization's meeting structure. Special announcements tend to raise both expectations and fears. The more normal the route of communication, the more people will take the initiative as a part of the normal business flow.

2. To satisfy *management*'s need, a 'Process Initiation Workshop' needs to be delivered to executives, managers

and key individuals who will be involved. This can be a one or two day event depending on the level of knowledge required to support the initiative.

The design of the Initiation Workshop should include the following topics:

- Definition of a process and how to map one.
- A review of the systems/process IPO (Input, Process, Output) model
- A picture of the business from a process perspective
- Descriptions of the types of process activities
- Descriptions of the types of requirements and the elements within each
- Decision-making and problem-solving methods
- Overview of the methodology
- Building in process quality

The workshop provides the managers with a basic understanding of the concepts behind process activities, the mechanics of the project, and the information–to communicate to their unit.

3. After fulfilling the above needs, and if an organization decides to develop the internal capability to conduct process-based activities, then an overall *technical training programme* should be implemented. The content of a technical programme is based on the competence requirements. These are reflected in a profile of a process consultant/facilitator built using the Core Competence Model of Hamel and Prahalad as shown on page 58.

Technical training programmes can be delivered in one formal programme of three to five days with review sessions at the end of each phase of the project to discuss best practices and special issues that have arisen or are anticipated.

The Structure
Establishing this element of the project includes:

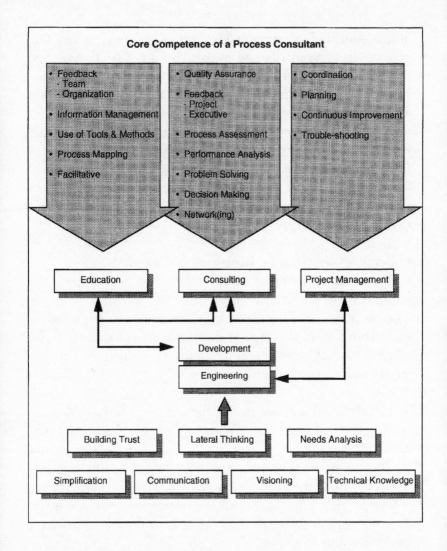

- Identifying the people who will lead, manage or have a technical role in the project
- Forming them into a team with specified roles and responsibilities
- Validating the project requirements and ensuring the managers of the project team members release them for the amount of time and effort required
- Establishing the communication, information and meeting

infrastructure.
- Establishing a centre of operations
- Establishing the ground rules, the levels of freedom and authority the team and individuals will have during the project
- Determining how the knowledge will be managed and transferred

Having these items established at the time of the project start-up keeps those involved in the project focused even during the later stages. Also, such proper front-loading prevents possible delays in the project.

The Project Contract

The final element in Phase 1 is to formulate all of the agreements and commitments on a team and individual level. In this sense a contract is a symbolic one. It can be designed by the team itself to convey their mutual support for one another to meet the challenges of a process project.

The articles a team might wish to include in a contract may cover:
- confidentiality
- boundaries
- deliverables
- what resources are needed and who will provide them
- response times to project team requests
- values
- feedback from and within the team
- mutual support and back-up
- role expectations

The contract can act as a source of accountability. In many cases early commitment and enthusiasm fade and there needs to be something more that holds the team and the project together. In addition, within the organization, the people working within the project often receive pressure from their managers and colleagues about their time, information and 'what is it really about?' type questions. Under the pressure some team members can begin to withdraw. The terms of the contract may be what keeps them committed. If the team has had no experience working together, then it is recommended that the contracting be the last activity in a two or three day team building event.

The importance of the launch resulting from Phase 1 cannot be minimized. Discipline at this stage is required. The overall sequence of the process is to educate, inform and listen to those involved, establish a project structure and reinforce the organization's commitment in the form of a contract.

All process activities are unique; however experience has shown that by following a standard process methodology, any variations can be readily understood and managed effectively.

Many of the **tools and methods** used in this phase are likely to be on someone's office shelf or within the capability of an appropriate department. Tools which need to be selected and developed by this stage are:
• Process mapping technique
• Problem solving method
• Decision-making method
• Quality management method
• Visual management system
• A project management system
• A method for running effective meetings

This excludes the major requirements of the technical programme which would include:
• Consulting techniques
• Facilitator techniques
• Performance analysis
• Project management
• Business analysis
• Process assessment tools

It adds a great deal to the process initiative if internal expertise is committed to support the effort. For example marketing could assist in the communication effort within the organisation. The Initiation Workshop can be run by an experienced manager with instructional design assistance from the Human Resources department. The technical training usually requires the use of an outside resource whose involvement in the project will depend on the capability of the internal staff. The contract could be drafted, with a degree of levity, with the help of the legal department and a graphics department could help communicate items like visual management, quality and problem solving methods.

EXIT CRITERIA	
Initiation Workshop	_____
Technical training programme	_____
A business case	_____
Project requirements	_____
Readiness assessment	_____
Project team	_____
Communication system	_____
Centre of operation	_____
Team contract	_____
Toolbox	_____

All of the above activities can be formed into a set of **exit criteria** for each phase. The exit criteria allow you to track the project's timing, quality and overall performance. At a pre-set target date or when the criteria are met, a review meeting should be called to review how the project is performing to date.

In addition to reviewing the criteria a general debrief method can be applied. The project leader asks the group to list separately all of the plus, minus and interesting (PMI) elements in three categories: the process, the people and the product. Based on this the leader asks what needs to be continued, stopped and started (CSS) within each category. This is a simple format which supports the overall performance of the project.

Finally, a word about key **risks**. For Phase 1 they include:
- starting too fast or with too much urgency
- making the process initiative separate giving it a corporate name and not linking it into the core business
- under-involving or under-informing the stakeholders
- over-selling the effort as the solution to everything

As mentioned at the start of the chapter, the process activity is a tool. To implement it into an organization takes effort and it seems when the effort required is above a certain level, it becomes a programme of and by itself. You can seriously damage the chance of success if you make the effort bigger than required. To prevent many of the possible problems in process-based activities, management must keep it simple, focused and model the use of the tools and methods. Most importantly, just ask questions to support the effort. There is a lot of truth in the saying 'You get what you ask for.'

Once the exit criteria are met, the project can then move into Phase 2.

Chapter Five
Phase 2: Understand the Business Process

In the next stage of activity, Phase 2, the attention shifts from the project to the process itself. Hence the tools and methods now become business focused. The level of learning required is high and it is in this phase that an organization comes to face the implications of conducting a process-based project.

A detailed look at what information is needed and how you collect it is the focus of this chapter. The structure follows a similar format as in the previous chapter: we review the purpose, the product and the process by which work gets done, the list of the exit criteria, the tools required and the risks.

Phase 2 - Understand the Business Process

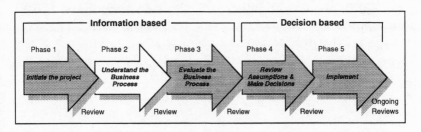

The **purpose** of this phase is to *collect the information* about the process which is necessary to communicate an accurate picture of how the process actually works.

The **product** is a *map of the process* with data on its current performance level.

The **process** within this phase has three elements: *Framing the process(es), Documenting the process* and *Assessment.*

The theme of this phase could be summarized in the word 'reality'. The information has to reflect the actual way the work gets done, not be copied from an outdated procedure manual or someone's hopeful perspective. There are a number of tools and practices which will be covered to ensure that the results of the effort are accurate and real.

Framing the Process

Once the processes have been selected by name, the boundaries of the activity need to be refined. Most people know what a budget process includes and what the document produced should look like. A survey can highlight issues and problems with the process. But making changes to a budget process is difficult until a set of parameters about the process has been established. The parameters are the descriptive elements such as size, shape, what is included and excluded. Once set, the parameters act as the frame for the process and allow the rest of the effort to be more focused. Here are some initial process questions that support the framing activity and have been known to humble many executive groups after announcing the name of a process to work on:

- What is the precise starting point and finishing point of the process?
- What is the actual output?
- Who is the customer of the process and who are the beneficiaries?
- What activities are included in the process?
- Whose involvement in the process will be documented?
- What does it cost to run the process?
- Is the process competitive?

- What value does the process add to the operation?
- What are the business (resource), management (operational) and customer (product) requirements of the process?
- What are the top three to five issues or problems with the process?

The answers to the above questions will allow a framework for the initiative to be established.

As mentioned in Chapter 3, processes are three dimensional. They are *linear* (starting and finishing points), they are *lateral* (cross-functional) and they have *depth* (how far down an organization a process goes). A process needs to be viewed from all three of these dimensions to frame it properly for the project.

In addition to the three dimensions, most organizations work in a matrix. Therefore a macro process will have to satisfy all three aspects of the matrix: Corporate, Functional and Working levels. Process activities are usually conducted in core processes but get implemented through the functional and working level. See diagram on page 66.

The Linear Perspective

It is relatively easy to form a *linear process perspective*. We are used to having a starting point initiated by input from another source. Still, a decision is needed as to whether or not to include that input as a part of a process. The same decision is needed at the end of the process when describing the finishing point. Where exactly do you want a process to end? With an output or do you include how the output is used in the process under review? It is analogous to throwing a stone into a pond. Is the starting point the throwing of the stone, or finding the stone, or the searching or the decision to throw? Is the finishing point the splash or skip or when the ripples subside or when you walk away? Determining these points are important first steps.

Many efforts use functional boundaries as starting and

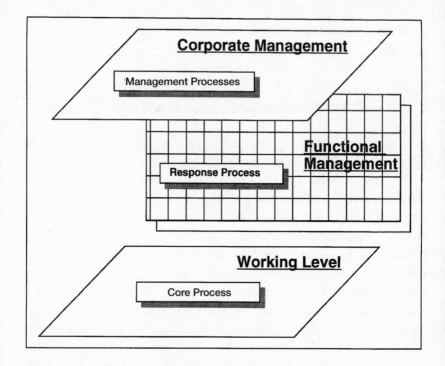

finishing points but like the ripples in the pond, processes do not necessarily end naturally at a given point. In fact the entire organization is one macro process when all the individual processes are connected. Experience offers the following recommended criteria, regardless of scale, for setting the starting and finishing points:

The starting point should be the tangible reception of items (an input) that trigger the process. It should be natural and make sense to those involved in the project.

The finishing point should be the hand-over of the product (an output) of the process to its customer.

Linear Perspective

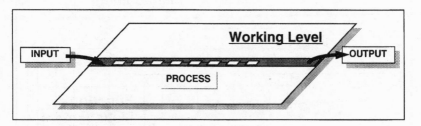

The Lateral Perspective

From a *lateral point of view,* how inclusive or cross-functional should the process be? For example, in the middle of the process, a form goes to finance for approval. Should you include what finance does with the form within the process? Or, a product is sent to a supplier for quality testing and analysis, should their activities be included in the core process map? It is relatively easy to identify what departments and who is involved in a process, but it is more difficult to determine which activities need to be documented and integrated. Based on experience, recommended criteria for determining inclusion into a process are:

- An activity has a mid-high level of impact on the performance of the process.

- Requirements of the process cannot be met without including the activity.

- The whole purpose of the activity in the other area is to support the process under study.

- The activity represents a loop, that is, it receives something from the process and has to act on it and return it.

At a more complex level, there is the concept of process interdependence. The question here is when to combine

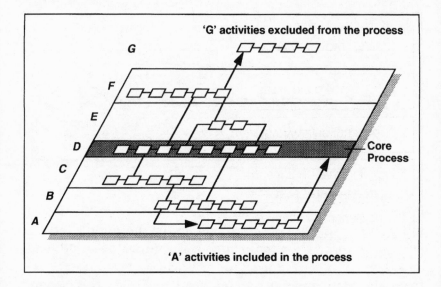

'G' activities excluded from the process

Core Process

'A' activities included in the process

processes into one larger process? From a process viewpoint, a company can be highly fragmented, as was the case originally when we started to look at Air Miles and its thirty-two processes. To achieve greater organizational focus and alignment, it is important to decide to integrate a number of processes.

The criteria used by Air Miles, for example, included:

• The number of interfaces and the level of interdependence made integration logical

• The processes were parallel and functioned to deliver the same end product

• The processes were part of the same core business

In the diagram on page 69, five client-focussed processes were integrated into one client-managed process.

Another lateral issue centred around the relationship between core and support processes. Many support processes come

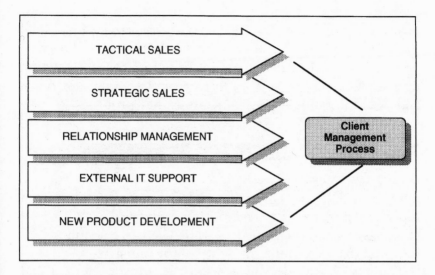

from the staff areas, e.g. Human Resources, purchasing, finance, IT processes etc. The nature of support processes is that they are likely to support more than one process, so they cannot be readily integrated and made part of any one process. Success has been achieved in our experience when:

- Support processes were documented independently and improved to meet the requirements of the core processes

- The support processes were clustered together in a group, so that overall cost and value to the organization could be calculated.

When a support process was 100 per cent dedicated to a core process, it was a candidate for integration.

These decisions about what to include in a process initiative can be made as the project develops. Often it is not until the initial process mapping is done that managers can begin to see the logic of including or excluding a particular process in a process initiative. At this stage of the project, a great deal of learning is taking place. Managers and staff are 'seeing' the process and the way the business works for the first time. From this new insight, adjustments to the project will need to be made. Even though a great deal of effort goes into setting up the project in Phase 1, process projects require flexibility and the ability to make adjustments as they proceed.

Depth

The third and last dimension of framing of process change is *depth*. The question is asked, to what level of detail do we operate and therefore document? Do we map what each individual does to a time and motion study level or do we stay at the 'process management' level? There are a number of elements that determine the depth of the initiative.

The level in the organization of the process sponsor is a determiner. Projects often reflect the sponsor's point of view and span of authority. Managing Directors or Presidents of firms may want to improve the performance of processes on a large scale. If they are the sponsors, the processes under study will tend to be large and strategic. The level of detail at which the project will operate will be macro. Management sponsored efforts will create a project which operates at a mid to micro level of detail.

A second element which impacts the level of mapping detail is who knows enough about the process to document it. If those knowledgeable are at level 2 or 3 of an organization then the project will operate at that level.

A third element that determines depth is the location of the problem. A process was documented at level 1 and the entire executive team had no problem with the result, but said that the problems were at next the level down. They then began the documentation at the deeper level.

In another example, a detailed map was created for an engineering company. When completed, the executive team agreed with the new process but indicated they needed a management level map because recent performance problems at that level were not easily seen in the initial map.

There is a fourth false driver to 'depth' decisions. It has to do with management assumptions. The dangerous assumption is that if you implement a broad process, then all of the sub-process improvements will be driven by the needs of the larger process. If you communicate the 'what' needs to be done then the 'how' it gets done will be a consequence. It is a dangerous way to approach process initiative.

There are many instances where a company has installed a high level process and it was impossible to implement because the map was not detailed enough. For example, at a large European automobile manufacturer, an engineering process had milestones, timing charts, exit criteria and quality gates. Management viewed this framework as the catalyst for change, but it became the catalyst of chaos. The process turned out to be a management process, not an engineering process. Any process initiative needs to document activities to the level needed to guarantee the successful attainment of the performance requirements. To do this an organization must ask how and where results will be attained from a process activity. The straightforward question is: 'Have we gone to the level of detail needed to understand key process issues and do we have the required level of information to make the necessary decisions to improve performance.' If not the depth of the project should proceed to the next level.

Once all three dimensions are defined, and the process boundaries established, the actual process mapping can begin.

Documenting the Process

Documenting includes three major activities: *Process mapping, Identifying resource requirements* and *Estimating resource consumption.*

There are numerous ways to document work flows and there are texts and manuals available to help. The method presented here is based on the systems IPO (Input, Process, Output) model as presented in Chapter 2.

When mapping each area or department gets a 'lane' so that if a process involves seven areas, the map will have seven lanes. All of the activities completed by that department are documented within the lane and all activities must be written at the same level of detail. This can be accomplished in a somewhat mathematical way. First you ask for a person or group to describe the process in 10–12 steps or activities. This is a level 1 map. Then for each of the ten, break them down into 3–5 steps which become a level 2 map and each of those in 3–5 again creating a level 3 map and so on.

The details are best collected in interviews which can be done individually or in groups. For high level maps and to document the interfaces, groups work well. As the desired level of detail increases or if you want to collect assessment data and suggestions for improvement, then individual interviews are the best format.

For each activity, the following format is used:

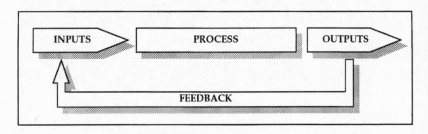

As shown in the workbook which follows, the top shape indicates the source(s) of input, the next shape describes the input, the rectangle describes the activity, followed by the output and where the output is sent. When cross checking and validating the map, the areas mentioned as the destination of the output, need to have indicated receiving that output as input to their next step.

A complete data collection format can be found in the appendix.

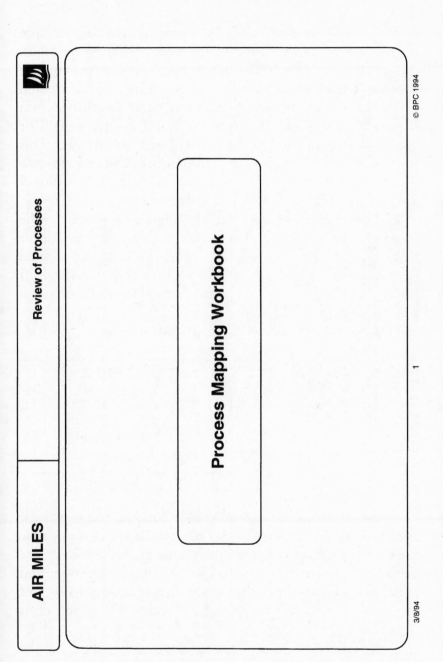

AIR MILES

Review of Processes

Process Mapping Workbook

© BPC 1994

3/8/94

1

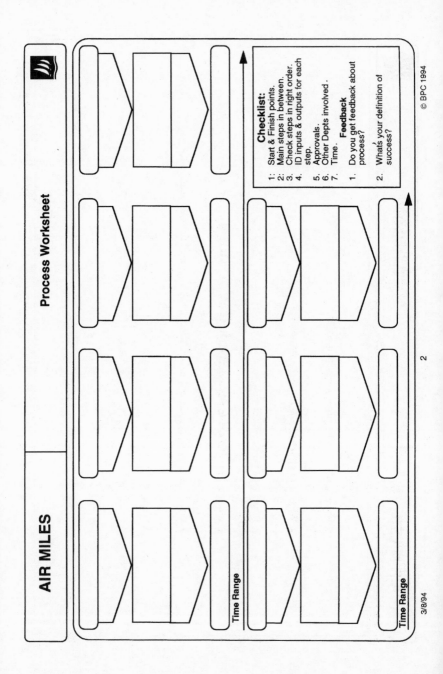

AIR MILES

Process Worksheet

Checklist:

1: Start & Finish points.
2: Main steps in between.
3: Check steps in right order.
4: ID inputs & outputs for each step.
5. Approvals.
6. Other Depts involved .
7. Time.

Feedback

1. Do you get feedback about process?

2. What's your definition of success?

Time Range

Time Range

© BPC 1994

3/8/94

2

AIR MILES

Process Overview

© BPC 1994

1. What is the starting point of the Process?

2. What is the finishing point of the Process?

3. Who is the customer of the Process?

4. What are the Resource Requirements? (Material, Budget, People, Support...)

5. What are Management's Requirements? (Quality, Time, Other targets...)

6. What are the Customer's Requirements? (Format, Time, Quality, Cost...)

3

3/8/94

AIR MILES

Review

1. Is this everything that happens? Did we leave anything out?

2. Looking at the map, what's your assessment?

Positives	Minuses	Interesting

3. What are your suggestions for improvement?

Continue	Stop	Start

© BPC 1994

3/8/94

4

Additional detail can be collected and documented. The man-hours and cost factors can be recorded on the map. Each step can also be coded. The y-axis of the map is time. For presentation purposes the time is relative. In working maps the time tracking should be accurate. A review of the one lane maps and an integrated map will highlight the major mapping points.

For Phase 1, a Level 2 map is all you need to begin to see the process and formulate opinions of improvement opportunities, waste, bottlenecks and the areas which are running efficiently. There will be a temptation to jump into resolving the problems, but all you have is awareness at this stage. Knowledge and understanding are required prior to decision-making and are the focus of Phase Three.

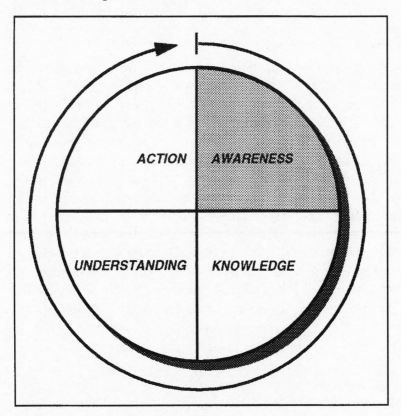

One of the most difficult items to become aware of is the identity of the *customer* of the process and to distinguish them from the *beneficiaries.* Identifying the customer is important because they are the source of the customer requirements. They have a prominent role in determining the content of the process. It is an interesting question as well. What makes it intriguing is that the goal here is to identify the *ONE* customer. The definition used that has stood the test of several projects is:

The *customer* of the process is the entity which receives the end product of the process and who creates the greatest value added with it.

Beneficiaries are any entities which receive information generated by the process or who receive the product of the process from the customer.

Many beneficiaries believe that they are customers. The situation is very much like writing a will. The 'customer' is the person for whom it is written, namely the courts with a set of legal and financial requirements. Those mentioned in it are the beneficiaries. Beneficiaries cannot specify what they want in the will, but they can ask the person preparing it if they would consider providing something to them. In process work, because information is available or generated from a certain point, people begin to make requests for the data. They then begin to make requests for changes, or for having different formats. Initially, the output of a particular step was designed to support a particular activity within the process. But if not managed, it balloons and the people on the 'copy' list become customers trying to be satisfied. Identifying customers and beneficiaries and communicating the difference is an important step whenever undertaking process activities.

Estimating resource consumption
After the process has been mapped, you can then begin to

tabulate what the resource requirements are to run the process. Items like *man-hours, IT costs, capital and investment items, material costs, cycle time, space, maintenance, flexibility* . . . the list can continue depending on the industry and type of process. In some organizations, the finance staff can be used to support this part of the effort. The resource calculations should have consistent time criteria: monthly, quarterly or annually.

It is also important to complete a cost interdependence picture. The question here is what impact does this process have on costs in the rest of the organization. Answers to this question are a critical part of this phase. Experience indicates that decisions or items within one process can greatly affect the costs of others. For example, while developing a process for an automobile manufacturer, to manage structural cost, it was found that 70%+ of the structural cost was caused or created by product decisions made within the product development process. It was the responsibility of the finance department to monitor and manage structural cost. Yet it was actually the marketing and engineering people who needed to learn how to manage structural cost by adding it to their decision-making criteria.

The cost interdependencies can also be calculated for the major outputs, both at the end and at any place a secondary output is produced during the process. Finally, with a well-documented map, it is easy to begin to tabulate value and non-value added steps and their associated costs to begin to set the future performance targets for the process.

Assessment: Resource requirements summary
This set of activities is the first step in setting the actual performance requirements of the process. Initially, the team working on the process determines broadly the overall performance improvement of the process. For example: *We can increase the productivity, quality and timeliness of the process by 25%* . . .

Then using the resource consumption data, the team estimates how much the resource level can be reduced in each category and reach the performance estimate of the process. This results in the second half of the statement *. . . reduce the resources required by 20%.*

A distinction needs to be made here between resource and performance requirements. They are interdependent and this relationship is something the leadership of the initiative needs to monitor. After the initial map is complete, you have the basis to evaluate the current resources utilization and predict future estimates. Performance targets will finally be set in Phase 3, after all the documentation is completed. When the final performance targets are set, you can then set the resource targets for reaching them. At this step we are identifying the potential, not setting detailed targets.

After the initial process map is complete, it will be the first time the organization may actually 'see' how processes work and are tracked, make judgements, and begin to think about how to improve it. In some organizations, a person(s) is assigned to handle all the enquiries and to run short briefing sessions if requested by managers. The data from this phase can also activate a number of communication channels and methods. Experience suggests that an important medium is visual management, with the appropriate tools including:

- the process maps
- spider charts or graphs with resource and performance data
- information about the process, its role in the business and the people who support it
- an education section about process activities and methods
- other data describing the goals of the initiative.

This system can be displayed either in a public place or a 'centre' where there is free access to obtain and share information.

The major **tools and methods** used in this phase are process mapping and visual management. In addition, an interview format for data collection is needed (see Appendix for a prototype).

Skills applied by the team include:
- Consulting techniques
- Interview techniques
- Performance analysis
- Business analysis
- Data integration.

As mentioned in Chapter 4, the process initiative is enhanced greatly if internal expertise is committed to support the effort. In this case, since the focus is on resources and their underlying costs, members of the finance staff would prove invaluable. Any specialists from within the process could also be used to determine the future potential and, importantly, validate the completed map.

All of the above activities can be formed into a set of **exit**

EXIT CRITERIA	
Starting point and inputs	_____
Finishing point and outputs	_____
Customer of the process	_____
Beneficiaries of the process	_____
Estimated requirements	_____
Level 1 - 2 process maps	_____
Process validation	_____
Resource estimates	_____
Measurement criteria	_____
Management review	_____

criteria for each phase, as shown in the diagram on page 81.

At the end of every phase, the project should conduct a management review. An outline of the management review which could last from a half to a full day is shown in the following diagram:

- **Purpose:**
  To validate assumptions and requirements
- **Process:**
  1 day Management working session to:
  - understand the process map and performance data
  - generate findings from map analysis and performance data
  - determine the activities that create unnecessary work or waste
  - make explicit business assumptions behind the process
  - determine the 'best practice' business & process performance requirements
- **Product:**
  - A clear understanding of the Business Process at management level
  - Criteria for team to make reengineering decisions

It is essential for both the quality and the flexibility to make programme adjustments so that disciplined management reviews occur between phases. This helps eliminate the 'surprise factor' and maintains the management support.

There are key **risks** in each phase. For Phase 2, they include:
- Creating too large a process by integrating too many external effects beyond boundaries
- Collecting data in excess of what is needed to make the map and the decisions required at this stage
- Identifying the customer wrongly

- Mapping based on what people want it to be rather than reality

However, once the map has been built, the resources established to meet current needs and future performance goals, and a review has been conducted for management, the project can proceed to Phase 3.

Chapter Six
Phase 3: Evaluate the Business Process

In Phase 3, an even more in-depth look at the process takes place. Mapping is done at a more detailed level, the performance of the process is documented and problem areas are highlighted. The focus of the Phase 3 team is to determine what is behind the process: what makes it function the way it does. It is at the end of this phase that the actual performance targets are set which will determine the level of change within the process and thus ultimately within the organization.

Phase 3: Evaluate the Business Process

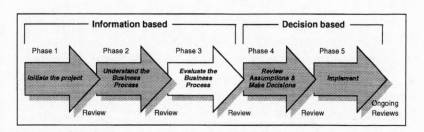

The **purpose** of this phase is to acquire the information needed to set the targets for the reengineering activity.

The **product** is a report outlining the current and future performance of the process, the areas which should be the focus of the reengineering activity and an understanding of what type of decisions are likely to be required to achieve the level of success desired. The report includes a Level 3–4 map of the process with appropriate highlights.

The **process** within this phase has three elements: *Investigating*, *Targeting* and *Planning*.

This is the last information phase prior to making the required decisions and the theme of this stage is 'pursuit'. In this case it is the pursuit of issues, reasons, assumptions, value-added, waste and other types of information which are needed to set the final direction of the project with confidence.

Investigating
In many ways the activities in this segment are a condensed version of Phase 2 but at a deeper and more detailed level. The project team must examine each step or cluster of steps in the existing map and identify the names of individuals and teams who perform that activity. In the event that the step is generic and many people perform it, it is then preferable to interview those who are performing at an above average level to get the benefit of their experience.

Level 3 mapping interviews can be conducted individually or in groups. The focus of the interviews is to document in detail how a particular step is completed. A way to begin is to ask the person responsible to take their work, break it into 5–7 substeps and then discuss each of them. This tends to provide a structure to the interview rather than asking the open question 'How do you do this?' The results needed from the interview are the performance details by the categories established in Phase 2. The major elements are:
- Input: what do you need to start?
- Cycle time: how long from start to finish?

- Effort: how many hours of people's time?
- Resources required: what materials or other cost-related items are consumed?
- Value-added: what does this step contribute and to which output?

In addition, performance indicators can be identified. They include:

- Quality: what is done to ensure work is defect free?
- Feedback: how do you know if you have been successful?
- Competence: what skills are required and do they exist at the required level?
- Authority and autonomy levels: where and what are they?
- Behavioural requirements: what does the process require people to do?
- Values: do the corporate values exist in the process and what values are present within the process?

Finally, during this Phase, experience has taught that a fully fledged assessment with suggestions from using the PMI (plus, minus, interesting) and the CSS (continue, stop, start) framework should be obtained. After the interviews, you will need to sum up the data for the process. The total cumulative cycle times, effort, costs etc., are calculated. A summary of the data relating to quality, behaviour, skills and other issues should then be prepared.

In the end you will have a map which you can colour code red (poor), yellow (marginal) or green (satisfactory) depending on the performance indicated in the interviews. Both the steps and the interfaces can be numerically and colour coded.

To validate the data and to get a picture of the entire process, it is often advisable to take a 'tour' and walk the entire process. This is a team event which will have members splitting off on different tracks to follow various activities with a rendezvous scheduled at pre-set process points. It may take one to two days to complete the tour. The key advantages of the tour are to see the work environment, make sure all interfaces are documented and to get a sense for how much of the process is based on formal steps versus informal ones. The deeper you investigate a process-mapping exercise, the more you will find that the work runs through informal networks. Although difficult to map, these often represent the most efficient way of completing an activity. These networks often change but have been established by the individuals involved as efficient problem solving loops. These cannot be mapped but should be documented in a general way: if you had trouble here, where would you go or who would you call? By documenting the ever changing informal support interfaces, you ensure continuity should a person move or leave a certain position.

As you are touring the process, you may find it interesting, if not vital, to collect copies of all forms, reports and documentation formats and note the type of systems used to provide data on the information network. Information Technology is an important aspect of a process activity and the use and support of an internal systems person is a valuable addition to a team at this stage. IT systems play an important role in developing or delaying solutions. For example, in the Air Miles organization a decision was taken to integrate two processes, because separate IT systems initially delayed the project's schedule for achieving results. The installation of a common system eliminated obstacles so that process changes could easily be implemented.

Information is a key output from any step and a requirement for effective decision-making. For example, in a recent review of information in a large German engineering organization that has been going through a number of structural changes, the two charts on the following two pages were developed to illustrate the challenges presented by IT in process projects.

Required Information	Source to Platform	Source Systems
Investment and Development Expense	• Finance Clerk in Platform (paper distribution 4-6 weeks)	- Plants Local IT System - Eng. Local IT System - Purchasing Local IT System - Supplier Local IT System - Eng.
Product Cost	• Finance	- Finance System
Standard Production Time	• Finance • Home Plant Team Meetings • Plants	- Local System - Paper - Separate local/national system
Timing (Release Details)	• Eng. (Internal) • Eng. (External)	- PATMACS System, Eng. paper - Local System
Quality Data	• Reliability	
Start Up Production Volume	• Corp. • Plants • Marketing & Planning	- Local System - Local System - Paper
Weight	• Eng.Chassis	- Local IT System or paper
Critical Parts Status	• Eng. Pilot Line Internal) • Product (External)	- IT System, Eng. paper - Local system

Information

Critical Parts Data
- APU Schedule
- KVI Status

Parts Release Status - currently release department held
- Internal Parts

- External Parts

Investment Status/ Tracking (not sum total but broken down into parts)
- Costs by parts/areas

Equipment Purchase Status, Timing Follow-Up
- Machine and Tool internal

- Machine and Tool external

Standard Production Time
- Time Status

Prototype and Product Development Status
- Engineering Hours
- Test Durabilty, Weight

Source

- Local System currently
- Local System currently

- Networked to Platform

- Eng. - PATMACS (Pilot-Tryout)

- Local System, System link after preproduction

- Finance system, Data from Line, Plants

- Eng.
- Plants ⎤ PROMIS
- Production Local System

- Plants System/ Eng. local system
- Finance System

- Eng. Local System
- Eng. Paper

This type of configuration is not uncommon. If different functions need to interface and improve any activity, IT will need to be an integral member of the team to assist in systems

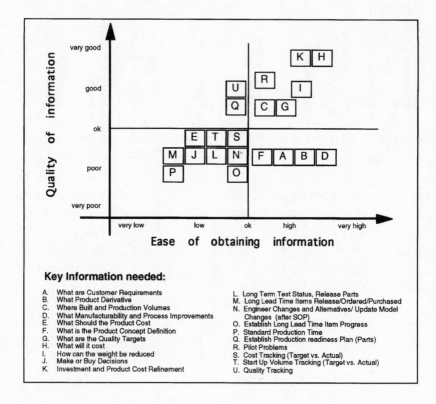

Key Information needed:

A. What are Customer Requirements
B. What Product Derivative
C. Where Built and Production Volumes
D. What Manufacturability and Process Improvements
E. What Should the Product Cost
F. What is the Product Concept Definition
G. What are the Quality Targets
H. What will it cost
I. How can the weight be reduced
J. Make or Buy Decisions
K. Investment and Product Cost Refinement

L. Long Term Test Status, Release Parts
M. Long Lead Time Items Release/Ordered/Purchased
N. Engineer Changes and Alternatives/ Update Model
   Changes (after SOP)
O. Establish Long Lead Time Item Progress
P. Standard Production Time
Q. Establish Production readiness Plan (Parts)
R. Pilot Problems
S. Cost Tracking (Target vs. Actual)
T. Start Up Volume Tracking (Target vs. Actual)
U. Quality Tracking

decisions, their costs, lead-time and impact.

A second natural outcome can be an assessment of information quality and accessibility. The diagram above is an example from the same engineering company.

Poor information quality impacts decisions, of course, but also can greatly affect the performance of the process. An excellent idea is to cross-reference the poor information and its source with the steps within the process. It will allow the team to see the relationship and estimate the impact on preparing the necessary decisions.

The investigation part of this phase requires excellent

project management. A great deal of information has been acquired and the team is learning at an accelerated rate. This is where the project infrastructure comes into play. If you have developed processes to manage and communicate the information and to document what has been learned for the team and for the organization, the project can continue to flow smoothly.

Targeting

At this stage the performance targets and expectations of the process are set. In theory, this is straight-forward. For each of the measurement criteria/categories identified in Phase 2, the team, directly or indirectly with senior executive support, identifies the performance requirements of the process. If it is an improvement project, targets could be in the area of 20–30 per cent improvement. If it is a reengineering project, targets in the range of 30–50 per cent are reasonable. If it is an architecture project, targets should be in excess of 50 per cent improvement.

The key issue in setting the targets is to *balance* them in advance. Experience has shown that you could achieve maximum cost savings if that was the only target. The same applies to quality, behaviour or man-hours. On an independent basis each could be reached only with some give and take in the other areas. But as mentioned previously, the requirements should include all critical categories:

Cost
Investment
Time
Labour
Quality
Behaviour
Information Management/Systems
Productivity
Price
There are often so many potential categories of

performance measurement, that the list must be prioritized and the top ones become the elements that trigger improvements in other areas. After the list of categories is completed and percentages or numbers are assigned to each item, the fun begins.

The simple question is: what do you want to achieve? And since you cannot have everything, how do you prioritize?

Some criteria include:

1. Take the highest priority improvement category and set a target (i.e. increase speed by 30 per cent)
2. Assess the impact of that target on the process (what might have to change to achieve the target and is it feasible?)
3. Assess the impact of that target on the other categories (what is the impact on quality, cost and effort?)
4. If the impact is deemed excessive or prevents improvement in other areas, then the target has to be adjusted (reset target for 20 per cent), then tested again
5. Repeat for second priority, then the rest in order

The team must always review the interdependence between the targets. In many cases, organizational compromises may be vital or considerations about the competition may cause one category to be dominant.

Experience shows that this type of discussion can be documented on a cause and effect diagram or a net mapping tool. But the relationships need to be recorded and made visible relative to the target. It is a learning experience for management and team to see and identify the performance inter-relationships between the criteria. It does bring the project down to reality. *It is at this point in the project that a quantum leap takes place from business review to business intervention.*

When the balancing of targets is complete and the realistic outcomes of the project are identified, the group can begin to identify possible scenarios for attaining the targets. Here we are providing a realistic direction. It is applying the double triangle described in Chapter 1 to this part of the project. The group now has a vision of the outcome, the mission remains clear, the likely values are in place. But, what is missing are possible strategies to guide the decision-making.

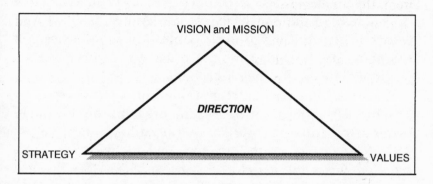

It is in this last portion of Phase 3 that the final pieces of information are formulated and incorporated into a plan. This plan outlines the possible impact on the actual running of the business that different decision combinations might have.

Planning
The ways in which a process can be engineered to meet the targets are extensive. The saying 'There are more ways to kill a cat . . . applies here. For example, to speed up the cycle time, you could:

- Focus on reducing the number of decisions
- Increase authority of lower level staff
- Automate a percentage of the operation
- Re-locate parts of the operation
- Focus on elimination of all non-value added steps
- Make the decision to out-source it.

All of these (and probably many more) are likely to be considered if speed or time is a factor. Again, the possible configuration of improvement options is something the organization needs to consider in advance. For example, if the decision was made to increase the level of automation, is it a *possible scenario*, given the investment and time it takes to realize the benefits? Is there an optimum solution possible? Are there areas (sacred cows) which should not be considered? In the previously mentioned case of the airline tender, re-structuring was not a viable option. So the team in charge needed to take a look at other ways to achieve the results and determine their acceptability.

What influences the acceptability of an improvement scenario is the impact it has on the organization. On more than one occasion, a senior group looked beyond the targets and asked: what might the organization look like if the targets are met? What will it feel like working here? Does the new process change the worker profile and the type of employee? These and other challenging questions need to be asked during this scenario planning. Experience suggests that an executive group may not like how any of the scenarios impact the organization and they may ask to make adjustments in the possible solutions or go back to the drawing board and start again.

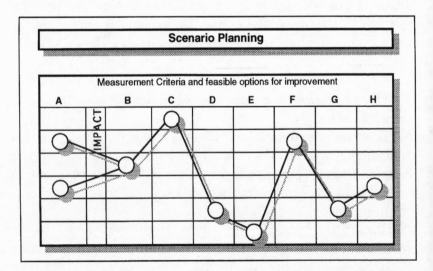

```
┌─────────────────────────────────────────────────────────────┐
│  ┌─────────────────────────────────────────────────────────┐ │
│  │            Scenario Planning Worksheet                  │ │
│  └─────────────────────────────────────────────────────────┘ │
│                                                               │
│  Process Name ..............................................  │
│  Measurement criteria ......................................  │
│  Priority ..................................................  │
│  Target & Reengineering requirement ........................  │
│  ...........................................................  │
│                                                               │
│  Options for achieving      Impact on criteria    Feasibility │
│  _____        _____       _____  │
│  _____        _____       _____  │
│  _____        _____       _____  │
│  _____        _____       _____  │
│  _____        _____       _____  │
│  _____        _____       _____  │
│  _____        _____       _____  │
│  _____        _____       _____  │
│  _____        _____       _____  │
│  _____        _____       _____  │
│                                                               │
│  Assessment of impact on other criteria                       │
│  Other criteria          Plus       Minus      Interesting    │
│  _____        _____     _____      _____     │
│  _____        _____     _____      _____     │
│  _____        _____     _____      _____     │
│  _____        _____     _____      _____     │
└─────────────────────────────────────────────────────────────┘
```

The contents of a scenario plan are illustrated in the worksheets.

The first is a summary sheet used to develop the scenarios. All of the options are entered on the sheet, and the group works from a pre-prepared sheet. There can be as many scenarios as the group wants to develop. A limited number of options (less than five) should be considered for immediate action. These should be entered on the second sheet documenting their impact on the various performance criteria.

If more pre-work is desired, a risk assessment can be

developed for each plan. Any risk assessment tool may be used. But consistent with the methodology presented here, a simple PMI can be applied. In addition, for each scenario, a CSS (what would be continued, stopped or started under this plan) can be applied to determine the impact on the process.

Many efforts develop wonderfully inspired lists of possible solutions, but they never see the light of day and thus end up as a great deal of wasted energy. As the Cheshire Cat in *Alice in Wonderland* said, 'If you do not know where you are going, it does not matter how you get there.' The above scenario plan tells the team both where to go and how they might efficiently and effectively get there.

Many of the same **tools** used in Phase 1 are applied here. They include:
- Process Mapping
- A Root-Cause or Cause and Effect Method
- Visual management techniques
- Project management tool
- PMI and CSS
- Scenario Planning Worksheets

By this time the core team should have become fluent in each of these tools and people involved in the project should acquire a level of literacy so that they understand the mechanics and can track the project.

The activities in Phase 3 are analytical as reflected in the list of **skills** required. They include:
- Data collection and analysis
- Facilitation/communication
- Performance analysis
- Planning
- Risk assessment

The information gathering portion of the methodology is now

complete and the focus shifts to making decisions. At this point the person in charge of the project could change from a team member with strong management skills to one with leadership skills. To push the process forward, strong influence skills will be needed.

The checklist for the **exit criteria** which, as usual, should be tested at a review session when this phase is finished includes:

EXIT CRITERIA	
Final map	_____
Performance summary	_____
Wall of forms	_____
Tour of the process	_____
Waste areas identified	_____
Final measurement criteria	_____
Final performance progress	_____
Scenario plan	_____
Risk assessment	_____
Management review	_____

There are key **risks** in each phase. In Phase 3 the major risk is the collection of too much information. The information need is obviously based on decisions. However, this in turn requires an understanding of the process. As the detailed mapping is undertaken, it is possible to go too far: as mentioned earlier, do not spend too much time on the informal processes, nor at the procedure level of detail. You can always go back to collect more data, but do not slow the project by getting bogged down in details.

Another risk is in the actual scenario planning. The plan is a framework for setting the direction of the decision-making. It is not the actual decision-making step. Thus the risk is that the scenario plan will limit the creativity and level of innovation. To manage this, the plan must remain only a strategy so that other options are always possible.

Another risk is that targeting can be unrealistic and the strategy daunting. Alternatively, it can be less than challenging and create a level of apathy. The targets should be given to a knowledgeable third party executive, who is not on the team, as a sounding board. In this way, the targets need to be challenging but attainable to maintain the level of motivation and interest required. After the completion of this phase, the group has the knowledge that is needed to reengineer the process.

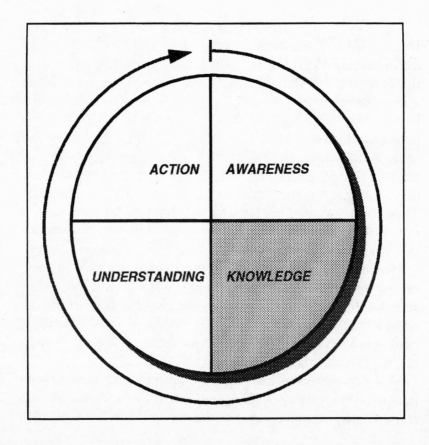

Chapter 7
Phase 4: Review Assumptions and Make Decisions

It has been stressed in the preceding chapters that the set of decisions taken in this phase will get the process to perform at the desired level. Decisions are a currency in a process-based activity. With them, you can acquire results and enjoy the benefits. Decision-making competence is essential in a process project and a major challenge, as the management perspective within the organization is often vertical, functional and limited. Budgets, planning, communication and reporting are departmental as are spans of control and accountability. Therefore, resources are allocated by department and much, if not all, of the infrastructure has a vertical focus. This way of thinking is, of course, challenged by a process initiative.

However, a prerequisite involves an executive group reviewing its own decision-making process. The team should start by determining the type and scope of the decisions the team is likely to make given the scenario plan. At this time, experience has taught that it is important to ensure the group has the executive mandate to make the needed decisions.

Many an executive team has developed cold feet at this time in a project, resulting in reduction of authority in the process team. Clarifying the level of authority in advance will ensure that the decisions made will be *aligned* with what the executive group is willing to allow. The team will then receive the support when *mobilizing* the required resources for implementation and this in turn will *accelerate* the final rate of achievement.

The activities in this phase require a focus on what flows through an organization, rather than on what flows up or down. Phase 4 outlines the requirements and the method for making effective process-based decisions.

Phase 4: Review Assumptions and Make Decisions

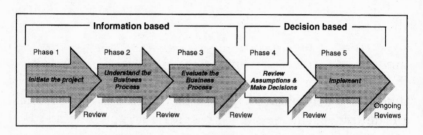

The **purpose** of this phase is to make the decisions necessary to have the process meet its performance requirements.

The **product** is a set of decisions formatted into an implementation plan which will meet or exceed the performance milestones set by the project team.

The **process** has four major elements: *Testing Assumptions, Process Workout, Decision Analysis* and *Implementation Planning.*

Testing Assumptions
The first concrete reengineering decisions that are made deal with assumptions. The group must decide on the set of assumptions under which the process will operate. Assumptions are often based on the perceived history of the organization and can be the hidden force of inertia within it.

The goal of this activity is to make them visible, test the validity and decide whether to keep, drop or change them. By definition: an assumption is a statement that is used as the premise of a particular argument but may not be factual and thus may not be otherwise accepted.

In organizations, people work in a particular manner either because of an explicit set of rules or policies or because they assume that what they do conforms with what is expected. Since process activities alter the way the work gets done, it follows that changing assumptions must precede changing the work.

For example, in a German engineering firm, executives discussed changing levels of financial approval to improve the cycle time. The group considered doubling the approval amount of a supervisor, but it had little effect on the process. The group then discarded the idea of altering the approval amount. When asked why, they responded that they assumed the audit department or the management group would never authorize more than double the approval amount. They were than asked to determine what approval level impacted the process positively. It was found that a six-fold increase from DM 500 to DM 3000 created the desired result. The group agreed, as a test, to challenge the assumption about approvals and went to management with the decision to increase the approval amount six-fold. The decision was accepted. Later the Managing Director's minimum level of approval was increased ten-fold. This simple decision story highlights the impact assumptions have on the capacity to make changes. Unless underlying assumptions are reviewed and challenged, decisions taken may not get the process to the desired performance levels.

The first step to reviewing, let alone challenging assumptions for the process is to define them. Experience suggests that the usual application of a root cause analysis or a cause and effect tool is ineffectual. In most cases, these two methods are applied to problems. Here we are trying to determine why something exists. Defining assumptions requires you start by agreeing that: *If that's the way the process is, then it reflects the way management wants it to be.*

Next, the team record their observations about the process and form them into assumptions. A standard list of observation categories is illustrated below. Any number of additional categories can be added. You must then take the observation and develop a number of hypothetical assumptions for further testing.

Process Assumption Categories	
Infrastructure	
decision making	problem solving
communication	information
People	
trust	teamwork
competence	motivation
Management	
priorities	expectations
Product	
quality	costs
Organization	
available resources	facilities
ability to change	values
Process	
control	department roles
efficiency	effectiveness

For example, take an item like 'control'. If there are many control steps (i.e. approvals) in the process, the team surmises that: *control is important.*

Secondly, they develop a set of hypothetical assumptions: *if control is important, then management must not trust its employees;* or *the competence of the staff is such that control is necessary;* or *management is basically insecure;* or *the complexity of the related product requires control.*

The number of assumptions should be limited to five per observation and the final list of assumptions should also be limited, although lists of twenty to thirty are manageable and not uncommon.

Once the master list of assumptions is created, a half to one day review session can be held and each assumption with its conclusions reviewed. The group can then make a simple choice:

1. the assumption is valid (yes, control is important)
2. the assumption is partially valid and needs modification (control in selected process areas is important)
3. the assumption is not valid and a new assumption is accepted (control is not as important as trust in employees)

It is by changing assumptions that you open the door to innovations and dramatic improvement opportunity. Altering assumptions allows new thinking to begin and ideas to be surfaced. The list of assumptions and conclusions concerning the process needs to be communicated to those participating in the project. The list acts as a tool to release creativity and enhance the first time quality of the decision by providing new criteria for evaluating decision-making options.

Process Workout

The workout is a three, five or possibly seven day decision-making event. It is during this programme that the process is altered to meet the requirements. By this point the team is aware, has knowledge and truly understands how the process functions. The action required is the actual improvement, reengineering or architecture of the process by making the decisions considered in the earlier phase.

The team has the following required information:

- Process maps
- Existing performance data
- Management requirements
- Business requirements

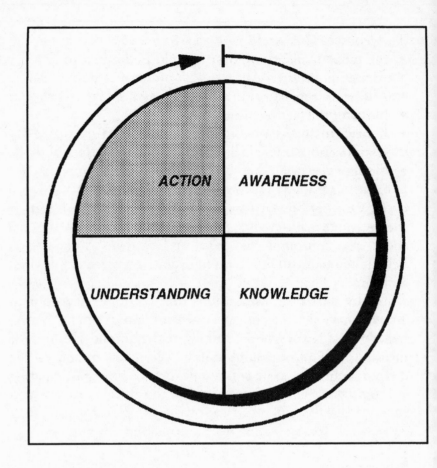

- Customer requirements
- Measurement criteria
- Performance targets
- Risk assessments
- Improvement scenarios
- Improvement strategy
- Operating assumptions
- Problem areas identified
- Interview data on recommended changes
- An array of tools and methods
- Accountability and authority to act
- Experience with the process

The ground rules for the session are:
- No recommendations, decisions only
- All decisions are actionable
- All decision-makers must be at the session
- No after the fact reconsideration
- If performance target is not reached by the end of the session, another is scheduled
- No sacred cows

Experience suggests a number of options for the workout event. One option is to conduct it in an intense format where the decisions made are based on the information available and the work is continuous until all decisions are made. The major benefit of this approach is that you can make more decisions at a more detailed level. Another option is a programme whose format calls for a day of decision-making and a day for testing the risk and feasibility of the decisions. The major benefit here is that there is a great deal of confidence in the decisions taken forward if they are pre-tested.

Two sample programme designs illustrate the differences.

Five day programme

	MONDAY	TUESDAY	WEDNESDAY	THURSDAY	FRIDAY
AM	*BACKGROUND* Background information - map - management review Detailed review of map Review of assumptions	Set up "base" in workplace Test decision 3 x team reviews at:- 10.00 12.00 15.00	*GREEN TAG* Detailed review of "updated" map (consequences of Day 1 decisions) Analysis of "green tag" delay areas Develop "type" cluster Review system "targets" Brainstorm list of solutions Formulate decisions	Set up "base" in workplace Test plan 2 x team reviews at:- 11.00	*QUALITY* Review definition of quality Define and select quality elements Estimate current quality performance Identify "source areas" of quality problems Identify root cause possibilities Select "target areas" and brainstorm possible solutions • 12.30 Management Review
PM	*RED TAG* Analysis of "red tag" areas Develop "type" clusters Review "targets" Brainstorm list of solutions Evaluate impact Formalise decisions • 17.00 Present to Mgt. Review (Mgt. indicates CSS)	• Validate decisions • Adjust map • 17.00 Present to Mgt. Review (Mgt indicates CSS)	*CUSTOMER REQUIREMENTS* Review customer requirements If requirements are not reached identify other areas for potential improvement Brainstorm "possible ways" to meet requirements for the future consideration (prioritize list) Develop measurement criteria Develop implementation plan RASI • 17.00 Present to Management Review (Management indicates CSS)	15.00 Validate plan Update map • 17.00 Present to Mgt. Review (Mgt indicates CSS)	*SYSTEM REVIEW* Detailed review of "updated" map (consequences of Day 3 decisions) Conduct entire "system review" (flow - focus) Evaluate impact of all decisions on performance targets If performance targets not reached identify other areas for potential improvement Brainstorm "possible solutions" for future consideration (prioritize list) • 17.00 Present to Management Review (Management indicates CSS)

A key item to notice is that the agenda is built around the target priorities identified in Phase 3. In this case cost was the first priority followed by quality, time and customer satisfaction. The highest priority leads the programme should the agenda slip and all topics not get fully covered.

An alternative three day design includes the Monday, Wednesday and Friday activities. It does not include the real-time testing of decisions done on Tuesday and Thursday. During the session decisions authorized by the group can be entered on the decision chart (see sample below) and the changes to the process are held. After reviewing the decision, its complexity is assessed, as is the scope of the decision, level of investment required and how long it might take to implement. Estimates as well as ratings may be used. What is required for successful implementation is the focus of the estimates.

DECISION CHART

Decision	Complexity	Scope	Investment	Time
A	High	3 units	High	6 months

After the conversion to a decision, the expected impact is calculated against the measurement criteria and a running total or performance score is maintained.

IMPACT CHART

Decision	Criteria A	Criteria B	Criteria C	Criteria ...
Total Impact				

This method should be repeated for each decision. In many cases, one decision will contradict a previous decision. If so, the group has to work out a solution.

A feature that can be added to the workout is a 'Devil's Advocate' period, where any new ideas or radical challenges can surface, re-surface and be reviewed. The learning accelerates, as do new ideas and even though you have a scenario plan, time for spontaneity can be incorporated. In a number of workouts, it is during these times that the breakthrough ideas are created.

The session should be very dynamic and be held in a facility within the organization. In this way, if a question arises or if someone wants to visually check how a decision will impact an area, they can go immediately to the workplace to get the data they need so a decision can be taken.

The end product of the workout is a map of the reengineered process, a list of the decisions to get there and the impact each of these decisions will have on the success of the initiative.

Decision Analysis

This set of activities involves the team reviewing the quality of the decisions individually and as a graoup. It is also a problem prevention activity.

Such a review carries some risk with it in a workout: you get a new process and you know what you must do to get there, but is it possible? A couple of worksheets should be used 'live', meaning, as each decision is made, it is recorded on the worksheet and the implications reviewed.

The first worksheet (below) requires the team to identify the primary area, who must implement the process and what area will be most affected by each decision. The purpose is to see where the burden of the implementation and the change lies and if the burden is too high on any one area. If it is, the implementation is off to a rocky start.

If a particular department has responsibility for a great many decisions, the team must question that department's

DECISION REVIEW WORKSHEET EXAMPLE

Place an 'X' to identify what area has primary implementation responsibility.
Place a 'Y' to indicate the area whose support is essential to ensure
  implementation success.
Place a 'Z' on the area most affected by the decision.

Decisions	Departments								
	A	B	C	D	E	F	G	H	I
1	X	Y	X		X				Z
2	Y	X		X		X		X	Z
3	Y	Y	X	Z	X	Z	X	Z	X

capability to manage that responsibility during implementation. In many cases, one department is seen as the source of
all cures (i.e. IT areas: let's automate everything). However, in
this case the calendar of IT projects is buried under a new list
of priority A projects. The department will not be able to cope
or the projects will be scheduled and worked on in due course.
The same situation may occur if a department is the source of
support too frequently and finally if one area is constantly
mentioned as affected, can they tolerate that much change?

As the list of decisions grows in the workout, the team must
be aware of potential impacts in this way. The consequence of
being on the responsibility or support list too often is that you
may require additional resources for the implementation and
not have them. Or if your department is on the 'affected' list too
often, maybe a more significant re-structuring or re-
organization is required. The project team must focus equally on
the process and the organization to achieve a balanced solution.

This type of decision worksheet can act as a visual
management tool and prevent the team from getting into a
mental rut during the session. If the first ten decisions all
involve the same department, is the group's thinking looking
for the same solution over and over? It would indicate that
more lateral thinking is needed. Occasionally asking about

why a department is not checked in any of the three categories might indicate that the group is overlooking that area as a possible source for solutions.

An interesting facet of the workout sessions is that the decision-makers are the participants. They see the impact of their work immediately. There is no delegating to be done. If an area not represented in the workout starts appearing frequently as support or affected, then a member of that staff should be invited to attend the session.

The second worksheet allows the group to estimate the resource requirements of their decisions. It can act as a pre-planning tool usually after the workout, but it could also be a guide as the decisions are being made. For each decision, estimates of what will be required to implement the decision are discussed and recorded. A participant represented can calculate

RESOURCE REQUIREMENT WORKSHEET FOR DECISIONS				
Decision	**Type of Resource**			
	Time	Capital	Labour	Material ...
1				
2				
3				

a running total of resources from their area and cry 'help' if the burden gets too high or outside their capability to deliver.

Much more elaborate worksheets can be used. Experience suggests that in many cases it is best to develop a computer spreadsheet. Each of the Type of Resource areas could be subdivided. For example, 'material' could be broken down by type as well.

Another attribute of this method is that by keeping a running tally, the group can see the cost of the implementation. Caution needed in this case centres around two facts:

- In initiatives like this, the costs are fixed and known while the benefits are just promises waiting to be fulfilled
- The project is likely to have a 'return on investment target'. The costs versus benefits can be monitored on a decision-by-decision basis

The last step in this decision analysis involves assigning responsibility for the implementation of each decision. A worksheet called a RASI Chart is effective for this. Under the 'R' you list the name of the person responsible for the implementation who can be held accountable. Under the 'A' is the name of anyone who needs to approve a decision. The 'S' list is the names of those who need to actively support the decision and the 'I' list is those who must be informed. When this chart is completed, the team is ready to prepare for the implementation.

Implementation Planning

This final set of activities develops a plan based on the 'logic of implementation'. Like most plans, it can be made simple or complex depending on the level of detail required. The key requirement is to develop a rationale based on a set of criteria. The assumption is that you cannot implement all the decisions at one time. Keep in mind that in addition to the process decisions, there is a communication and education component to deliver so that the organization is prepared for the implementation.

In a moderate sized project, there are likely to be over 100 decisions which need to be implemented and the results tracked. It is recommended that the team use the following criteria as the basis of the logic:

- Implement decisions sequentially in process terms. If you divide the process into thirds or quarters, the team should first implement those decisions involving the first segment of the process, then the second, and so on
- Within each portion of the process, there will be decisions

that impact the *core* of the process and others that improve the *support* areas like reporting activities. Take the *core-based decisions first* as they may change the support needs

- Decisions which require a long lead-time may begin earlier. Many of these items require the development of people or systems in advance. Some may also require structural changes which may occur in line with the overall strategy. Alternatively, it may be that a decision is tied to an event in the corporate calendar (i.e. altering planning or resource allocation might need to wait until the next planning sequence)

- To increase the involvement of the organization, decisions which affect only one area can be implemented locally and used as platforms for learning within a department

Sequential implementation avoids duplication. Results achieved from an earlier decision may impact other decisions that follow. So by implementing decisions in succession, those that occur later in the process sequence will not result in unnecessary modifications.

Irrespective of whether you undertake process improve-ment reengineering or architecture, there are no significant variations in decision making. The scope of the decisions may be different and the impact may vary but the thought processes are fundamentally the same.

The **tools** applied in this phase include:
- Workout programme design with supporting worksheets
- Cause and effect method
- Visual management techniques
- Project management tool
- PMI and CSS
- RASI charts

The activities in Phase 4 are action oriented as reflected in the

following list of **skill** requirements:
- Decision-making
- Assessment
- Facilitation/communication
- Planning
- Risk assessment

Once the decisions are made and have been incorporated in to a plan that makes success attainable, the focus can shift to effective project management. To push that process forward, strong leadership and influence skills will be needed.

The checklist for the **exit criteria** which, as usual, should be tested at a review session when this phase is finished includes: In Phase 4 the major **risk** is the team's ability to work together.

EXIT CRITERIA	
Workout Programme design/delivery	_____
Assumptions defined	_____
Conclusions specified	_____
Assumption review session	_____
Master decision list	_____
Impact worksheet	_____
Decision review worksheet	_____
Resource requirements (by decision and totalled)	_____
RASI charts	_____
Implementation Plan	_____
Master timing chart	_____

As decisions are made and the impact felt, old political position-taking is common. The second major risk is that objectivity can be lost. If it is perceived that the decisions are arbitrary and not well thought out or if one person dominates the programme, then the results may be seen to be subjective or biased. A third area of risk is in the team's ability to estimate the impact of decisions. This team will probably set the schedule for implementation. If it under-estimates the impact of the decisions, support will evaporate quickly.

Finally, the decision-making element runs the risk of creating too grand a challenge by going for the improvement all in one bite. While certain situations warrant one bite, most process efforts require decisions that improve the process by both incremental steps and the much sought after innovative leaps.

At the end of this phase, having the list of decisions, the scenario plan, resource estimates and all other exit criteria met, the team now understands what is needed to create the new process.

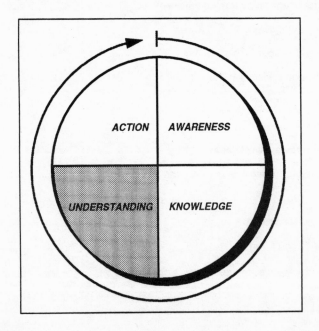

Chapter Eight
Phase 5: Implement

The implementation strategy discussed at the end of Phase 4 has its own set of supporting prerequisites. These need to be met, so that an independent implementation process can proceed. This chapter will present a framework for an implementation plan, suggest a support structure and discuss many of the potential pitfalls which occur in this stage.

Phase 5: Implement

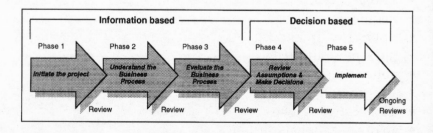

In this Phase, even though you are creating a new process by implementing decisions, the primary focus needs to be on people. The key to implementing the process changes is to identify those in the organization who can impact the activities which will be changed. Their disciplined adherence to the new process will make it work and allow it to achieve the targets that have been set out. If you can identify the support requirements of the key persons and meet them, then implementing process changes can be successful. It is people who are doing the implementing, they are not just affected by it.

The **purpose** of this phase is to identify and provide the support needed to ensure the success of an implementation plan.

The **product** of this phase is a process which meets all performance requirements.

The **process** within this phase has four major elements: *Education, Coaching, Tracking* and *Continuous Improvement (CIP)*. In addition, experience has taught that a *support infrastructure* should be developed and put into place before initiating any change. Items to consider include:

- a process support team of advisors
- a technical support team (e.g. finance, IT, human resources etc.)
- a process centre or war room
- a communication package and system
- a series of training packages for management, staff and those most affected
- policies supporting staff reductions (if necessary)
- a suggestion system
- an incentive system
- an organizational learning system (e.g. documentation)

Although this infrastructure is an integral part of this phase, elements of it probably already exist in your organization and others can be developed at the same time as the process activities develop. Since the contribution of each item in the infrastructure is critical, a review follows:

A process support team of advisors is a small group composed from the original team or from process competent individuals within the organization. They are the consultants to those implementing and their role is to educate, coach, track and measure.

A technical support team (e.g. finance, IT, human resources etc...) includes internal staff from the different functions who are trained in basic process skills and briefed on the project. Their role is to support the local implementation. They are specialists who can undertake financial modelling, provide IT support, or conduct a needs assessment.

A process centre or war room can be the heart of the project at least for the early days. It becomes the communication centre. It should include a visual management system, all project information and reference material. It could also be the training centre as well. It is usually operated by existing project staff on a rotating basis. Companies generally keep it open until the process is implemented and the skills have been transferred in the operation.

A communication package and system are part of the education element. Information that should be available to communicate or send upon request includes:
• Process maps
• Final copies of all of the worksheets used in the project performance targets and progress to date
• Reference material about the project and process
• Articles and packages distributed within and external to the organization

They should be in a packaged format suitable for managers, team leaders or staff meetings. Having one source keeps the message consistent and allows updated information (or success stories) to be easily distributed.

A series of training packages for management, staff and those most affected will naturally have a different focus for each audience. The core of each programme should be the same and should include process theory and concepts along with details about the project. For managers, though, the emphasis should remain on how to lead and manage processes. For team leaders and supervisors, continuous improvement (CIP) and process mapping can be stressed. For the staff and those in the operation, the programme can highlight teamwork within a process.

Policies supporting staff reductions (if necessary) may already be in place if it is anticipated that job losses will result. In many cases, the losses occur through buy-out and early retirement programmes. Still, it is laudable if other services, like out-placement, career counselling and re-training are available.

A suggestion system is a valuable tool. Since the process activity rarely goes to the job or task level, it is often up to the teams and individuals to apply the concepts to their set of responsibilities. In support of organizational learning and a CIP effort, a form of suggestion plan about process improvements and ideas can involve the entire organization in the process effort.

An incentive system is sometimes used to support achievement of the targets at a milestone or overall. It can simply be part of an existing scheme or it can be developed separately specifically for a process effort.

An organizational learning system is critical to the long-term success of the organization. Since processes are fundamental to the business, knowledge about processes and the way they work will be mandatory. This knowledge can be spread through constantly documenting success stories and having process leaders lecture or conduct group discussions on their achievements.

Taken together, these items form the bridge over which you will carry the process initiative. The stronger the bridge, the faster you can traverse it and the heavier the load it can handle. Furthermore, measurable results from organizations where we have helped to change processes indicate the more competent an organization is in process activities, the faster they can respond to changes in the market or the competition. Capability and the speed it takes to change processes will be equivalent to the capability and speed with which a company gets a product to the market.

Each decision implementation process has the four elements to it: *Education, Coaching, Tracking* and *Continuous Improvement.* To follow these elements, we can review the implementation of a particular decision, in this case in a large car manufacturer in the UK. Their parts operations had been divided into three segments. The portion under study was the release and sourcing processes. In the process engineering session, an issue surfaced around initial order quantities when new vehicles were launched. This problem included how orders were calculated and when final orders were to be placed.

The original process involved the UK parts department speculating on what car dealers would need and then placing their orders with the parts suppliers. The parts would be delivered to the warehouse awaiting dealer orders. If the dealer orders were less than the initial order, the UK operation was left holding excess inventory. If the dealer orders exceeded the initial order, parts would not be available for customers. When asked what was the formula for the initial order, the department manager indicated that playing roulette in Cannes was an equally valid method. When the dealers were asked how they determined their orders, they too were fond of the roulette analogy. The parts operation did not have a Just-In-Time process, so they tended to order in excess of what was needed just-to-be-safe.

As in many process projects, the final solution (being too logical and simple) was discarded at first. The decision which was taken is summarized as follows:

The dealers were guessing, but the dealers' guesses were firm orders to the parts operations. Therefore, it did not make a difference when the dealers placed their orders. So the team decided to move the dealer order date forward of the parts operations order date. As a result the guess work was taken out of initial order. Accuracy of the initial orders increased and the parts operation reduced levels of inventory.

Great solution. The process was changed, all of the worksheets completed and it was entered on the decision list to be implemented.

The implementation challenge was to get hundreds of dealers to accept the process decision. A PMI was done and it was noted that the decisions may adversely impact the cash position of the dealers. The answer to this obstacle was that the dealer delivery and payment date were unchanged and the warehouse had to set a schedule with the suppliers to maximize inventory turns.

The first implementation step taken was education. A sample of dealers were contacted about the project, the new process and the changes. All related information was shared and the dealers accepted the proposed changes.

Education
The fundamental question underlying the education element is this: Do people have the knowledge and understanding to support a given idea?

In our example, once the knowledge requirements of the dealers were identified, a training/briefing package was developed and delivered. The package highlighted the business situation, who and how they would benefit, what impact would be on all parties and how the action would be supported. The programme also outlined the project infrastructure and constantly solicited improvement suggestions. In too many cases, organizations 'sell' solutions. Honesty is a requirement of these programmes. Since the programme is about their process and business, they will either experience the reality very soon, or figure the whole picture out within a short period of time. Involve the people affected as much as possible in the learning process.

Coaching

Even when people know what to achieve, they do not understand how. Therein lies the need for coaching. The focus of the coaching is 'how to' make process changes. It is a support service that is both proactive and reactive. It is proactive in that the process team or a support person must actively contact those who are making the changes and ask them about their progress and or difficulties. If the progress is excellent, people are asked to share how they went about it and lists of best practices are developed and communicated. Coaching is reactive in response to problems. Once the cause of the problem is identified, then the proper tools and materials are used to resolve them. Problems and solutions are documented and communicated as a problem prevention initiative.

Those who are implementing the decisions must have a sense of ownership. Coaching requires a distance between the support person and the staff person needing assistance. In many cases, ownership is transferred to the person who knows the most. However, implementation should be considered unsuccessful if the workload still centres around the support team.

Tracking

Once the staff become process capable, the support team simply begins tracking the results and building a reference library of success stories and best practices.

Tracking requires the use of many of the tools and methods used in previous phases. Interviewing, analysing performance and conducting root cause analyses are the primary activities. The element is a 'hands-on' activity. Walking through the process and following up with those who were initially interviewed are the best ways of gathering accurate information. It is through this follow up that suggestions for improving the process are obtained. The key is to communicate that your role is supportive, not one of auditor.

One of the challenges facing a person in tracking is coping with the 'good news syndrome'. Most employees know that management wants to hear that the implementation is going well, so they will communicate only good performance data which will fulfil management expectations. One way of overcoming this is to conduct group follow-up sessions as opposed to individual meetings. In the group you will get a variety of opinions that give you a better picture of what is really happening.

One of the roles of the support team is to build process support networks within the organization. In these follow-up sessions, the support staff should encourage the group to work together to solve process problems and provide them with the necessary tools. This is the first step in creating the capability to do Continuous Improvement in the operations.

Continuous Improvement (CIP)

CIP is the primary vehicle for institutionalizing process initiatives. These activities can be facilitated by members of the support team, but it can be even more effective if local management would lead these improvement efforts. CIP requires the use of support tools, particularly in visual management. People need to see the results of their efforts to get a sense that they are responsible for the performance of their unit. There must be a working environment of autonomy and responsibility for this activity to be successful.

No matter which of the three types of process activity was initiated (Improvement, Reengineering or Architecture) CIP becomes the process improvement method. It is in going through this cycle during the implementation phase that a culture of improvement is created.

The major **tools and methods** used in this phase are the training packages, problem solving method, visual management and an information management system. By this time the staff should have become process literate and be capable of functioning independently.

Skills required of the team include:
- Consulting techniques
- Interview techniques
- Performance analysis
- Business analysis
- Data integration

All of the above activities can be formed into a set of **exit criteria** for Phase 5 and include:

EXIT CRITERIA	
Specified infrastructure	_____
Education packages for executives, management and staff	_____
Continually updated process maps	_____
Performance feedback sub-process	_____
Regular project review meetings	_____

There is no end point of this phase. Debriefs and management reviews should be incorporated into the normal meeting process within the organization. When the process is meeting all of its performance requirements then the operation has adopted the process as its own. You can then use their process capability in new ways. These are described in detail in Chapter 9.

The key **risks** in Phase 5 include:
- loss of interest by management in particular. Often projects are abandoned if they do not show immediate results. But in process projects, each decision has its timetable and it is easier to hold management accountable for implementing a decision rather than a process

- uncoordinated follow up by the support team. This is also a project killer. If one area is held to task and is being disciplined, and the neighbouring unit is not, eventually people ask 'Why us?' and their enthusiasm withers. This is particularly true of larger cross-functional projects.

- commitment and resources being withdrawn. If the implementation plan is too aggressive and consumes resources at a higher than expected rate, management will sometimes withdraw the level of resources to keep the project in check. It is a better strategy to re-visit the plan and adjust the timing of it

For process initiatives to be ultimately successful senior staff have to begin to manage process and be held accountable for process performance. It is the commitment of the staff and the project team that will lead to the achievement of the goal.

Chapter Nine
Process Applications

An organization's process competence is developed by going through the full cycle of a process-based activity. If the project scope is large and the company's investment significant, there will be a process capability that can be redirected. There are areas where applying process tools and methods can enhance the performance of a business. Creating new process-based solutions to business issues is a key application where a company can receive a return on its process investment.

There are a number of situations where process can be a part of the solution:

- Creating new processes
- Developing process-based training
- Documenting informal processes
- Resolving urgent business issues

Creating new processes: This activity refers to establishing new business processes in response to new organizational situations or markets. In an era where market and competitive forces are constantly changing, there is a need to determine how to respond effectively and efficiently. In the case of Air Miles, they placed a number of operations into a new function that did not previously exist. This function had no precedent and there was no experience in determining how to best run the new type of operation. The traditional response is to assign a manager with some form of related experience and make it his or her responsibility to launch the new unit. The result is that each of the separate activities run separately in an uncoordinated fashion. The assumption seems to be that if the parts work, the whole is OK. This is not always the case.

Using the same tools and techniques from the process activities described in this text, a group at Air Miles was formed to develop a process from a clean sheet of paper. Each of the activities was mapped, interfaces were agreed upon and built into the process, as were levels of authority, decision points and quality gates. The team set their own performance targets and made sure the new process met them. Even after creating a new process for the unit, they ran a shortened process improvement project to ensure that the result was excellent. This group effort was possible because of the competence built into the organization.

There are many opportunities of creating new ways of doing things. These opportunities are probably created daily in large organizations. For example, a multinational organization is opening up operations in China. The Western work processes are not suitable and new ones need to be created. Whenever there is a merger or acquisition, the need for new integrated processes is created. In a recent acquisition project, the two sales organizations used the basic tools and methods to create a new process as opposed to having one organization impose its process on the acquired company.

There are endless opportunities for using elements such as:
• process mapping
• process assessments
• decision-making frameworks
• risk analysis
• testing assumptions.

When a process project is completed, a method of organizational learning needs to be established and training programmes or modules created and tailored to the different constituencies within the organization. If what was learned is allowed to waste away, the organization loses additional benefits that are possibly worth more than those achieved in the initial project.

Improving Types of Processes Other Than Business Processes
Much of the focus in the process arena is on core business processes and key support areas. There is another category of process which can be called *management processes*. These include items like meeting processes, performance appraisal processes, decision making, policy making and other management leadership activities. Applying process methods to these areas can greatly enhance overall management performance. Recent projects have included:

- developing a *leadership transition process* as a tool to ensure a consistent, high quality transfer of authority. It has been used for positions as high as the chief executive for European operations and with key positions within sensitive areas. In this project, stating policy or providing guidelines was insufficient. The best management practice for leaders was documented and a process built, assuming new positions. This has been added to the management toolbox.

- the executive board of a multi-national organization found itself with an agenda filled with non-strategic items which should have been handled lower down in the organization. A decision was taken to create an entirely new *meeting process* which controlled where decisions were made simply by establishing entry criteria for agenda items. The result was a standardized meeting system, not just a better meeting process, which forced decisions to be made at the desired levels.

- another decision related process application was in the area of national versus European autonomy. In this case the process tools and methods were used to document how key decisions were made in each of the main functions (manufacturing, sales, human resources, finance etc). The goal was to clarify and establish the boundaries of autonomy for the national companies for this European multi-national. The result was that the decision-making process became consistent for each function within the national organization and the overall relationship between these local companies and the European headquarters was greatly enhanced.

At the root of each of these projects was a process element which was best served by these organizations applying their acquired process competence originally gained by conducting a process-based activity.

Training applications

In a number of organizations, the tools and methods described in process projects have found their way into training programmes. For a large merchant bank in London, a programme developed to improve their key corporate account management skills, process mapping was used extensively. The purpose was to solidify the link between process and behaviour. How they managed relationships and the underlying process were inexorably linked. As in this programme, process modules/tools can be incorporated in every type of development programme. In a team building course, the group was asked to map the team process. Having it on a wall, rather than discussing what they remembered, greatly accelerated the learning curve of the group and the programme became over-subscribed after this process module was added.

In addition to modules, entire programmes can be

developed to build an organization's process competence. A typical five day programme to develop skills to a practitioner level might look like this:

Day 1: Defining Business Process Activities
- Definitions
- Explaining reengineering to your organization
- Reengineering challenge
- A process activity model

Business Trends
- Industrial Engineering
- TQM
- Process
- What's next?

Process Strategy
- Assessing current process strategy
- Determine value added of process activities
- Establishing and prioritizing requirements
- Organizational readiness

Day 2: Leading process activities
- Personality of process
- Process requirement and styles of leadership
- The courage to make decisions

Day 3: Core method
- Sizing the process
- Process mapping
- Scoping the current process
- Value added analysis
- Assumptions
- Classifying the type of process activity
- Measurement criteria
- Identifying the opportunity
- Risk assessment

 - Management reviews
 - Decision making
 - Piloting

Day 4: Benchmarking
 - Why use benchmarks?
 - Selecting companies
 - Collecting data
 - Developing conclusions

Planning Implementation
 - Process within a process
 - Business case
 - Infrastructure requirements
 - Decisions one by one

Day 5: Process Applications
 - Training
 - New Frontiers
 - Strategic problem solving
 - Building a core competence

Process skills have more applications than just Business Process Reengineering projects, and having the tools and methods institutionalized by integrating process modules into existing training or developing skills through specific programmes are excellent ways to improve organizational performance.

Business Issue Applications
A strategic application is to use process tools and methods to resolve key issues. Mapping the way issues are and how they can be handled provides an objective backdrop to discussions and/or negotiations. Issues where applications have been successful include:

- product allocation, where some production facilities felt that there was a national bias towards particular countries and that the allocation was too subjective. The allocation method was 'mapped', installing objective decision-making criteria at key points.

- a modernization programme, where there was no learning from a previous project and mistakes were being repeated. Previous decision methods were mapped and new ones developed. In addition the earlier project process was documented, analysed and the new processes immediately applied with savings in the hundreds of thousands of pounds

- relationship management, where the loss of a key client was imminent. The organization used process as a platform for improving the relationship. By jointly (with the client) developing a process to meet the client's requirements, trust increased to the level required to maintain the relationship. In this case, the process became the tool to achieve customer satisfaction.

All of these applications represent ways of using process methods and tools in new ways to improve performance. To limit their use to BPR projects, or tie them only to IT projects is severely limiting their potential value. If they can be incorporated as tools for management and staff, then the goal of organizational learning in the process discipline can be achieved and the success of future BPR projects enhanced

Chapter Ten
Case Study

SUMMARY

OF A

PROCESS ENGINEERING CASE STUDY

Crunch Time

© BPC 1994

Table of Contents

2

134

BUSINESS BACKGROUND

© BPC 1994

This summary of a case study involves a process project with an emphasis on quality. It illustrates the thinking at each stage of the project and the results ultimately achievable.

One of the world's largest auto manufacturers has two major design centres, one in the USA, the second in Europe. The European Engineering Development Centre is considered to be "international" in that it is responsible for the design of all vehicles which are distributed outside North America. For over 4 years the Engineering Development Centre has been attempting to implement a standardised vehicle development process. This has proved extremely difficult, as the complexity of the current vehicles, the process itself, and the changes in culture are significant barriers.

BPC assessed the situation and gained agreement that concurrent to the macro process implementation, which can only be done with the initiation of a new vehicle (i.e. a 1998 vehicle), lower level engineering processes needed to be improved. It was felt that processes for vehicle system and sub-systems were still too large a platform to make rapid changes to gain performance improvements. It was determined that at the component level, the teams involved were under 100 persons and made process activities feasible.

Components are divided into 3 groups:

    carry-over, which are components that are simply used in the next vehicle with no change and receive no budget allocation;

    modified, which require limited reengineering and are allocated small budgets

    new, which represent new applications of technology or are new products in themselves.

The new components are allocated large budgets and have the highest impact on the quality of the vehicle. It was decided to focus on the development process for these new components. In a new vehicle there are 2000+ components. Of these 10% or 200 are new. These 200 + components all differ in complexity and different development methods are used, ranging from outsourcing, traditional specialist teams and an integrated project centre .

For any of these approaches there exist major vehicle milestones which must be met, but there is no common process engineers follow in any of the approaches to develop the components. The development process was managed by enforcing deadlines and milestones that had to be followed. Since there was no common process at this level, problem prevention, and other improvement efforts had no sound basis from which to work. The major challenge facing this project was to determine if a common process could be developed encompassing the different approaches and if not, to develop an alternative to meet the management, business and customer requirements.

135

Business Summary

Improvements were required in the following major areas:

Product related:

Product Cost, Development Cost,
Capital Investment

Quality
- history of excessive cost overruns (1993 - $100 million)
- delayed release of the most recent vehicle due to quality problems = lost revenue of $ 1Mill. in Germany alone

Performance
- the warranty problems are a constant surprise

Process related:

Development Time,
- schedules slide and then 150% effort in last 6 months disrupts other vehicle programmes, creating the same effect in the next programme..

Productivity
- artificially maintained due to heavy outsourcing

People related:

Support the new culture
- move from a functional to an integrated way of working

Use of new skills and methods
- 1950's methods were still applied to build 1990's vehicles

Level of interdependence and team-work - required from departments and supplier

© BPC 1994

Summary of Requirements

- Integration of ongoing efforts/initiatives into the development process.
- Incorporate methods and tools for overall improvement (e.g. Systems Engineering, Quality design, Continuous Improvement, Training, Visual Management, Problem Solving).
- Create a Core Process which contains all quality elements used by engineers.
- Apply all current resources and functions where they have the most leverage and potential contribution.
- Use the final process as a "Platform for change" to a quality-driven culture.
- Apply the standard 5 Phase BPC approach *

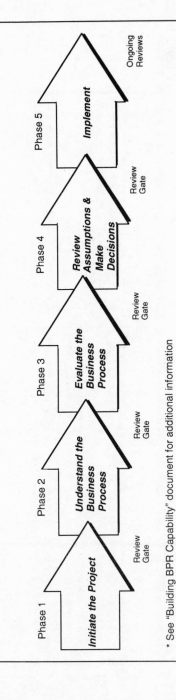

* See "Building BPR Capability" document for additional information

© BPC 1994

5

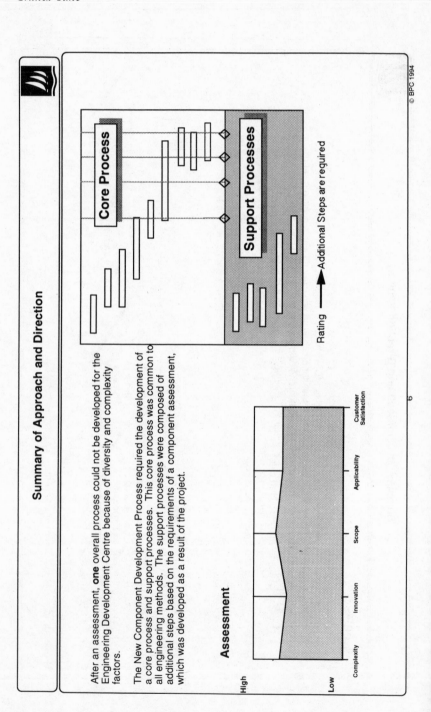

Summary of Approach and Direction

After an assessment, **one** overall process could not be developed for the Engineering Development Centre because of diversity and complexity factors.

The New Component Development Process required the development of a core process and support processes. This core process was common to all engineering methods. The support processes were composed of additional steps based on the requirements of a component assessment, which was developed as a result of the project.

Core Process

Support Processes

Rating ⟶ Additional Steps are required

© BPC 1994

Assessment

High

Low

Complexity   Innovation   Scope   Applicability   Customer Satisfaction

Summary of Approach and Direction (cont...)

BPC's Approach:

- **A.** Study Process Component (5/93 - 9/93)

  This case highlighted the issues, and a business case for proceeding was created with a complete set of requirements for the project. The major result was a prototype process. Four new components were selected from a current car programme which was due to be launched in late '95. The components represented differing types and scope. They included a new engine, a safety, an electrical and a mechanical component.

- **B.** Pilot new process on 4 current components (11/93 - 5/94)

  Performance versus the requirements was calculated and the result was a validation of the project as the business issues had in fact become more critical. The map in this case was partial, as the vehicle was still incomplete. However, using the completed map from the previous vehicle, workshops were conducted to make the process alterations needed to improve the performance for the rest of the development cycle. The results of this, although encouraging, did not significantly reduce the problems. Over 60% of these problems resulted from having no process in the earlier stages. Major result was the acknowledgement that one single process was not viable and a core process with support processes was needed.

- **C.** Apply the new process to support the development of a new vehicle which began in May 1994 for launch in the Fall of '98.

  The new process is being readily accepted because the actual process was developed by the Engineering Development Centre engineers and the Engineering Development Centre believe that they could achieve savings of 7 - 10 % of development cost and capital investment for each new car programme. That translates into savings of DM 40 -60 Mill.

Mapping Summary

The Team mapped the 2+ year development cycle detailing the activities and relationships for each of the departments and suppliers. This led to the creation of a 20m x 2m process map. For ease of presentation, this map was broken into Quarterly Summary maps like the one shown below:

Process Safety Component (Phase A)

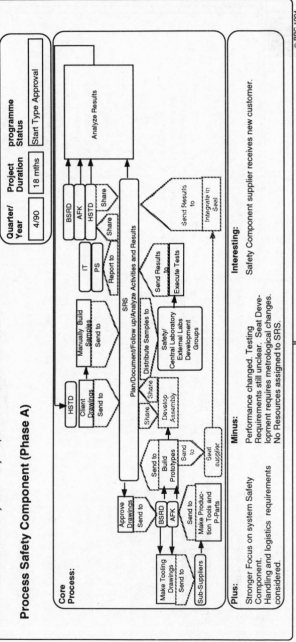

Quarter/Year	Project Duration	programme Status
4/90	18 mths	Start Type Approval

Core Process:

Plus:
Stronger Focus on system Safety Component. Handling and logistics requirements considered.

Minus:
Performance changed. Testing Requirements still unclear. Seat Development requires metrological changes. No Resources assigned to SRS.

Interesting:
Safety Component supplier receives new customer.

© BPC 1994

8

140

Mapping Summary (cont...)

For the same Quarter major events / milestones were also documented with improvement suggestions

Process Summary Safety Component - Timeline

Official Nomination of Suppliers Customer	First Production parts	First Sample Approval Parts	Need for Logistics Requirements	Need for Handling Requirements	Inability for NJC to assemble Safety Component

→ Time

Remarks/Considerations :

The inability of NJC to assemble the component resulted from missing handling and logistics requirements. The fully Product Engineering controlled supplier chain leaves all the responsibility with Product Engineering unless it is defined clearly.

Recommendations :

Continue: Executing First Sample Approval Tests before SQA does it.

Stop: Controlling the complete supplier chain.

Start: Stating Suppliers roles and responsibility clearly in the beginning. Aligning the complete supplier chain before production tooling.

Quarter/ Year
4/90

Summary of 4 Components

Component	Engine	Security	Chassis	Safety
Timing	Beyond Platform Scope	Crash programme	"Normal"	Follow No Go for earlier car programme
Project Scope	Assembly in Europe Different Developing Suppliers for crucial components.	Configured off the shelf components with Adaptations in Body Department required	Black Box Part in close cooperation with highly experienced supplier	Detail controlled part and process with separate developer and completely inexperienced manufacturing supplier
Product Complexity	550 different parts/3 derivatives 3 full platforms	low component complexity all platforms concerned	low complexity, 1 derivative, one platform	low complexity, one platform
Innovation	high percentage new components and technologies	low	low to medium	medium
Organisation	Project Centre	Distributed in Body and Electric	Chassis	Interior
Responsibility	Centralized in Project Center	Central for Electronics	Central in Chassis	Central in Safety Restraint Systems
Authority	Coordinating Function	Limited to Electronics	Coordinating Function	Limited to Safety Restraint Systems

© BPC 1994

10

142

Project Summary

From the start, the Engineering Development Centre had all of the quality tools at its disposal.

However, it did not have the processes in place to maximise those tools.

Hence, the New Component Development Process was initiated. Its primary focus was problem prevention.

By preventing problems early on, Engineers felt that later "firefighting" would be reduced. Engineers could devote more time to quality enhancing activities.

The types of quality activities include:

- Building Quality Framework
- Identifying Quality Pre-requisites - Overall Logic
- Identifying Types of Quality
- Conducting Quality Process PMI - Summary (Example)
- Conducting Quality Process CSS - Summary (Example)
- Documenting Quality Process Issues

Examples summarising the above activities follow.

Project Summary (cont...)

Quality Framework

The following is an example of the Engineering Development Centre's quality matrix. A key decision was where prevention ends and problem solving begins.

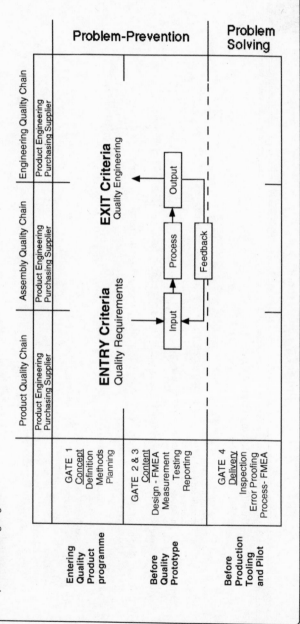

144

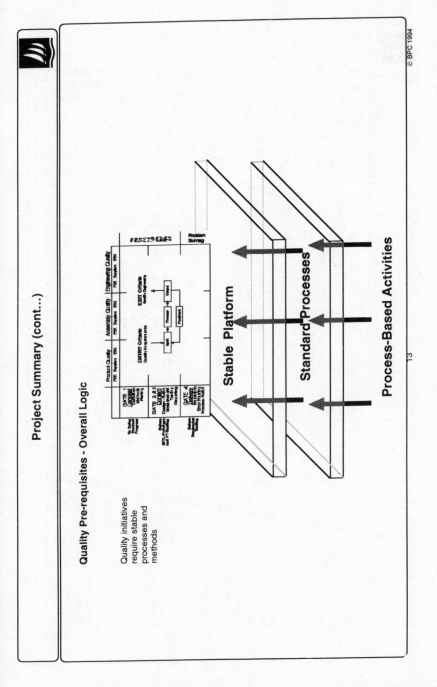

Project Summary (cont...)

Quality Pre-requisites - Overall Logic

Quality initiatives require stable processes and methods

Stable Platform

Standard Processes

Process-Based Activities

© BPC 1994

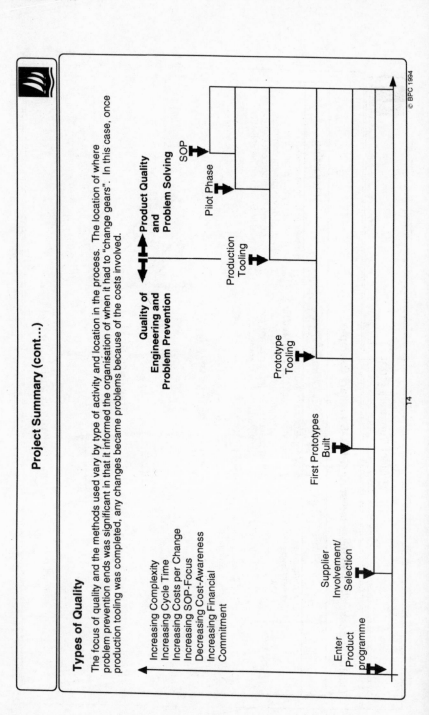

Project Summary (cont...)

Types of Quality

The focus of quality and the methods used vary by type of activity and location in the process. The location of where problem prevention ends was significant in that it informed the organisation of when it had to "change gears". In this case, once production tooling was completed, any changes became problems because of the costs involved.

Quality of
**Engineering and
Problem Prevention**

→ **Product Quality
and
Problem Solving**

Increasing Complexity
Increasing Cycle Time
Increasing Costs per Change
Increasing SOP-Focus
Decreasing Cost-Awareness
Increasing Financial
Commitment

Enter Product programme

Supplier Involvement/ Selection

First Prototypes Built

Prototype Tooling

Production Tooling

Pilot Phase

SOP

© BPC 1994

Project Summary (cont...)

© BPC 1994

Quality Process Plus-Minus-Interesting (PMI) -Summary Example

	Plus	Minus	Interesting
Process	Low complexity Involved Suppliers Early	Proj.-Engineer assigned Everything has to be approved by Management, late resources allocated to Project Engineer, too many Variations in manufacturing and assembly	The way to be innovative No developing Supplier, Only Individual development contracts. Engineering Development Centre involved in Sub-Supplier Selection
Quality	Highly Innovative Requirements defined and Stabilized	Component focused No Performance Requirements or Test Specifications Logistics and Handling not considered Requirements change	Corrosion Protection is not standard requirement Durability of 10 years defined by Plant Official Release of Quality specs was halfway into programme
Cost	Low Costs for Changes	Cost-book overdrawn High number of changes after Tooling Process Variations require additional Tooling	Early Cost-Book Overdraw didn't stop the process
Timing	Low cycle Time SOP was met	Informal Process of Innovation was Driven into Phase II Late for First Prototypes Assembly at Safety Component Supplier not possible	Manufacturing requires reduced performance requirements

15

Project Summary (cont...)

Quality Process CSS - Summary (Example)

	Continue	Stop	Start
Process	To have one link between Engineering Development Centre and all participating parties; the Project Engineer	Starting Projects without adequate staffing.	Requesting Performance and Target descriptions at Product programme Entry. Documenting the process in one format. Debriefing projects.
	Add staffing and descriptions of the goal of the development effort to the Entry Criteria for starting a project. Give job descriptions and project management training to Project Engineers.		
Quality	Engineering Development Centre to perform First Sample Approvals before Quality Assurance does it.	Entering concepts without requirements into Product-programme. Seeing suppliers as manufacturers. Rating Test-Results OK/ NOK without criteria. Testing for understanding	Requesting Performance and Testing Criteria early. Using IT for better information exchange. Stating standard requirements (i.e. 10 years durability/ corrosion protection)
	Establish Quality-Gates to evaluate the determinators of engineering quality between the core processes.		
Cost	Using Suppliers Testing equipment	Testing outdated prototypes. Variations in manufacturing and assembly processes. Taking responsibility for every action. Last Minute Changes.	Reporting and tracking budgets on a component level . Including suppliers in the Idea refinement process. Developing a clear defi-nition of the goal. Using IT for continuous project tracking.
	Request component focused budgeting and reporting of development costs and capital spendings. Request spending report		
Timing	To work with external specialists on an exclusive basis from the beginning.	Dealing with Sub-Suppliers. Approving every Decision.	Clarifying the system-supplier/ supplier relationships earlier. Clarifying and delegating responsibilities to suppliers and engineering companies. Using IT to reduce time losses.
	Give Development contracts and reduce involvement with Sub-Suppliers. Break down the exclusive start of production-focus.		

© BPC 1994

Project Summary (cont...)

Quality Process Issues

Quality-Determinators	Types	Examples		
Errors	Omission	I Forgot! i.e. Corrosion Protection		
	Commission	Commit to Change without complete validation (testing) of impact		
Engineering (Drawing) changes	Before Tooling	Single-Tube to Double-Tube	146 SBT Indices Quality of Engineering	
	During Prototype	Non-Return-Lock, Bowden Cable, Buckle		
	After Production Tooling	Sensorhead, Seat Attachment, Tubes, Buckle	397 SBT Indices Product Quality	
Costs	Cost per car	Door Check Link, Target: Cost neutral, SBT Overdrawn before Prototype		
	Development Costs	"Money is a matter of a handwritten memo"		
	Capital Investment	Process variations require multiple tooling		
Information/ Documentation	Accuracy	Usability/Legibility of documents		
	Completeness	Test-Results and Status-Reports/Meeting Minutes, Drawings		
Process	Repeatability	Knowledge-Transfer, Carry Over, Position towards partners		
	Standard	Reduction of variation, Locking Lever, Assembly		
Timing	Delay	Too few Prototype cars before Pilot No Assembly ready for Pilot		

Summary of Targeted Results for New Component In 1998 Vehicle

Based on the new process the Engineering Development Centre has high confidence that the targets will be met.
A tracking and visual management system is established to document and communicate the following goals:

- Quality targets exceeded at each stage.
- Development, investment or material costs below budget.
- Development time reduced by 20 % while meeting all required ISO 9000 criteria.
- Development cost budget met or below production price.
- Cycle time per problem resolution reduced by 25 - 50 %.
- Warranty costs of New Components reduced and measured by % of warranty expense.
- Increased success in testing and validation
- Non productive material cost drops.
- Speed of implementation and level of user satisfaction to be rated as excellent when measured in 6 month intervals
- A reduction in production tooling measured as a percentage of overall change.
- New Components will meet all technical specifications in the prototype built.

It was felt that these efforts will yield savings of $40-60 million dollars in their new programme.

18

150

Summary of Significant Findings

Within the Engineering Development Centre there exist formal and informal processes. The project documented the formal processes. Many of the improvements made resulted from converting the informal processes into formal processes. However, a lot of the work does get done through personal networks and non documentable processes.

- The Core Component Development Process is supported by informal processes which cannot be

  - reengineered
  - controlled

- The Informal Processes are based on

  - networks of relationships in the working level
  - level of trust
  - locations within the Engineering Development Centre
  - experience of the participating parties

- The Informal Processes interface with the Formal Processes where

  - Networks do not exist
  - Information is delivered/required from a formal process such as
    - Approval/Control processes
    - Downstream Processes with a different level of formalisation

The informal processes have to be recognised and their contribution estimated. Organisations must determine what percentage of the work must follow formal or informal processes. The final percentage is a reflection of the culture of the organisation.

© BPC 1994

19

Summary of Significant findings (cont...)

- Knowledge transfer needs to accompany product transfer for quality to improve. These transfers can be accomplished by using functions as "Resource Centres" of expertise.

- Functional borders are no longer rigid if recommended process changes are implemented.

- Roles and responsibilities evolved over the life of the project, hence requiring continuous flexibility.

- The progress of the process mainly depends on functional cooperation. Lack of process controls had elevated simple timing questions to the level of Director at the Engineering Development Centre .

- Testing is mainly done at vehicle or system level. Resources have to be re-allocated to fully test the component before assembly.

- Risk analysis (point of no return) was done only at the project start, thus the project could not be stopped without tremendous cost. Risk assessment needs to be conducted at various milestones or gates (stages).

- To meet cost, the engineering team was willing to reduce assembly and functional reliability. Decision-making priorities were installed.

20

Summary of Significant Findings (cont...)

A major issue negatively affecting cost and quality involved **Engineering Changes**. Hence, it was critical to understand the root of the problem and the location of the root within the process.

The amount of costly Engineering Changes increased dramatically the later the following requirements were finalised:

Initial Requirements resulting from
- Management's decision at Concept Approval

Additional Requirements resulting from
- Learning about the Design
- Gathering experience from Manufacturing and Assembly

Systems Requirements resulting from
- Interdependence of Components and their Interfaces
- Experience from Tests on System and Vehicle level

External Requirements resulting from
- Management Decisions to add new legal requirements
- Changing option packages
- Adding export markets
- Changing Performance Requirements

Thus to minimise costs, it was critical for the New Component Development process to identify and confirm the above requirements as early as possible.
This required that all participating parties in the Development Process such as Developing Suppliers, Engineering Support Companies, Purchasing, Manufacturing Engineering etc. are considered members of the project team.

This resulted in a cultural change.

21

Decisions Example

Error Type	Example	Process decisions integrated to eliminate error	Responsible
I forgot to inform	Engineers don't know about latest changes or test results.	Make diagram of all functional Interacts with other components. Find out who is responsible for other component. Apply list to every change and test.	Project Engineers
I received wrong answer	We need ±12 V between the seats vs. we install a safety system that requires wiring	Ask the right question. Describe the problem to the engineer responsible, not your intended solution.	Project Engineers
We didn't know we had to do this.	Transponder arrives without code because nobody was assigned to do that.	Form a development team with all downstream and crossfunctional customers inside and outside the Technical Development Centre. Define and document roles and responsibilities in the beginning.	Project Engineers
This is the result of a management decision.	DOHC -> SOHC injection system: Temporary cancellation of Safety Comp. development	Execute FMEAs to point out risk involved in decisions before escalating issues. Present results realistically without fear to be the messenger of bad news. Do not make a decision without complete set of information.	Development Team Line Management Platform Management
We didn't know before.	Lack of experience with explosives	Identify lacks of experience and knowledge and form development team that knows. Identify list of critical issues and attack them first. Don't test against what you know first. Collect and document downstream and crossfunctional requirements actively.	Project Engineer with AP Development Team
It takes too long until ...	Bottlenecks in central labs, lack of resources and equipment for component testing.	Develop a validation plan and communicate it so that resources can be allocated or sourced. Specify the purpose of tests on the work order form so that only the feature in question gets tested. Identify the processes and CIP them together with the players involved.	Development Team Project Engineer Development Team w/ admin areas

© BPC 1994

22

Decisions Example (cont...)

Error Type	Example	Process decisions integrated to eliminate error	Responsible
Component used not up-to-date	Large numbers of components get ordered and stored and rebuilt.	Build a Validation Plan. Collect Timing of interacting components. Schedule Component Built Program. Order smaller numbers.	Project Engineers with Prototype Shop
Unrealistic test requirements	Old and permanently added-to test procedures	Challenge existing Test Specificatons against new component requirements.	Development Team and Central Lab
I didn't get response in time	Requests for feedback and feedback get stuck in forwarding chain.	Communicate on the lowest possible level. Use voice mail and Lotus Notes. Ensure your department knows, when you are where and when you will be back.	Development Team
There was not enough time.	Decision and approval processes delay progress.	Leave the budgets allocated to the project with the project -> Not every order has to be approved in the financial approval chain. Streamline the development cycles before problems require you to do so. Define and document the information and material flow processes in the beginning based on the technical structure of the system and the supplier chains used after SOP.	Engineering Development Centre Finance, Line Management Development Team
		Validate changes with engineer responsible for interacting component before executing them.	Project Engineers
We had to change it back	Wire routed through drilling for attachment of a bolt.	Validate changes with engineer responsible for interacting component before executing them.	Project Engineers
No time to document	Important documents get written after SOP.	Use standard formats and tools (IT) that make documentation and distribution easier.	Project Engineers supported by Programme&Advisors
"They" haven't yet...	Production volumes for optional components late.	Communicate your requirements to other departments as soon as you know them. Do not assume "they" should know.	Development Team through Project Engineers

© BPC 1994

23

155

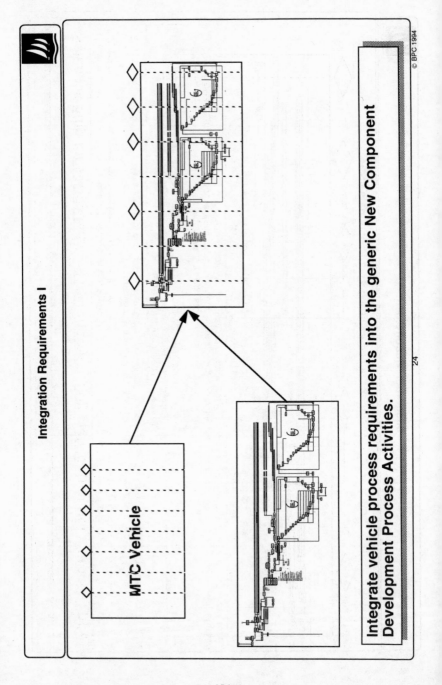

Integration Requirements I

MTC Vehicle

Integrate vehicle process requirements into the generic New Component Development Process Activities.

© BPC 1994

24

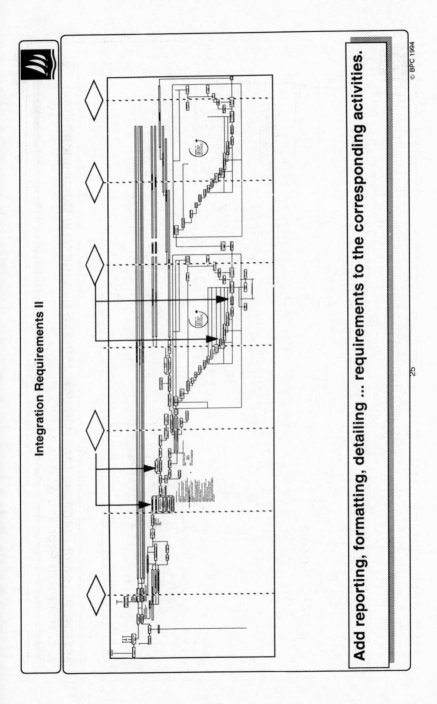

Integration Requirements II

Add reporting, formatting, detailing ... requirements to the corresponding activities.

© BPC 1994

25

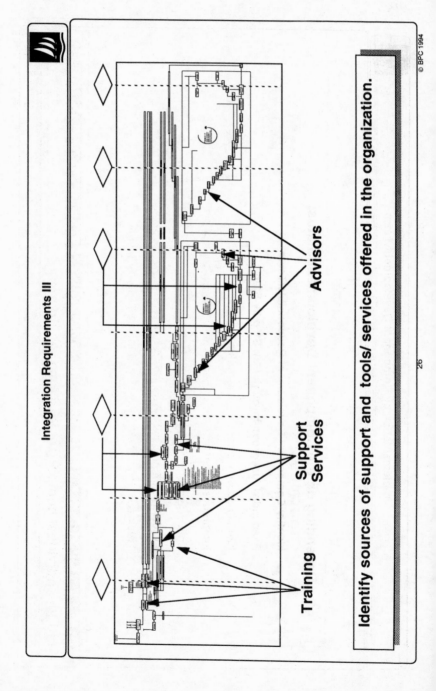

Case Study

Implementation by Component Development Team

Depending on the Component Development Status:

Identify Component Development Responsible/Team

Read individual/group through Map Step by Step

Identify support needed in executing the steps

Integrate support schedule into the development project plan

Catch up with missing project steps

Execute remaining process steps required

Track and document progress and incorporate learnings

The implementation will be driven by the development schedule of the vehicle and the individual component lead time requirements.

© BPC 1994

27

159

Implementation

The keys to implementation are the responsible engineers for the estimated 200 new components of the vehicle. They were the customer of the initiative and it is their disciplined adherence to the new process that will achieve the potential results. Therefore the implementation requirements of the project are synonymous with the requirements of the engineers to use the process.

The steps of the implementation are as follows:

- Conduct a one day development programme for each of the 200 engineers in groups based upon the lead time of their components. The programme would:

  » explain the new process

  » outline the benefits to them in using the process

  » identify how it contributes to problem prevention and the quality of the vehicle

  » explain the structure of the support services that they will receive

- Set up the support structure until the last production tooled component fulfils all requirements. The structure is as follows:

  » Process support will be provided through the Training-area. Their role is to provide the process education, the coaching and CIP advice. The staff required (estimated at two full time people) to support this activity will be provided by the consulting company.

  » People support will be provided through the Training-area. Their role is to provide technical education coaching and ACIP advice. Primary focus is on existing Training tools and methods.

  » Product support will be provided by the Engineering Development Centre advisor network. Their role is to provide quality and engineering tools and methods support.

  » Suppliers support will be provided by Purchasing. A point person has to be assigned. The person's role is to collect and document all suppliers issues and coordinate assistance in the resolution.

  » Engineering Development Centre support will be provided through the traditional management and platform structure. Areas where support may be required include Finance, IT, HR.

© BPC 1994

28

Implementation (cont...)

© BPC 1994

Delivery of support services:

Goal of the support activity is to ensure the disciplined adherence and the Continuous Improvement of the new process.

The two members of the support team would:

- conduct initial training for the component team including suppliers. If suppliers enter the program later it is the responsibility of the support team to brief the suppliers in the new process.
- meet with each responsible engineer once a month minimally. This would increase for components that had high quality risk.

The half hour meeting between the support person and the project engineer would be to discuss the progress, document problems or obstacles, and collect suggestions for improvement. In addition they would inform and make the connection between other support functions and the responsible engineer depending on the type of problem identified.

There are three major benefits:

- At the completion of the vehicle program we will have a proven world class component development process and support structure which can be used with every new component in both major and minor programs.
- What is learned from long lead items can immediately be incorporated so that future components would be using an already improved process.
- Problems are identified sooner and the support required is utilized earlier.

As a management tool each component could receive a flat pin on a master visual management tool to track the progress of all components. In addition they could be color-coded regularly to reflect their performance. This could be broken down by functional department.

The result would again be earlier detection of problems and the earlier use of any or all prevention and resolution tools.

29

Appendices

Business Process Consulting, Ltd.

PROCESS TRACKING WORKBOOK

Daily Follow-up of Vendor Materials

PROCESS MAPPING EXERCISE

PURPOSE

° Understand current operations and how they work.

PRODUCT

° A "photograph" (Process Map) that clearly depicts all activities, identifies all tools used, and shows information and reporting flows as they actually happen.

° A complete documentation of what is done at a step by step operational level.

PROCESS

° Map activities.

° Review for accuracy.

° Adapt until the Map reflects reality.

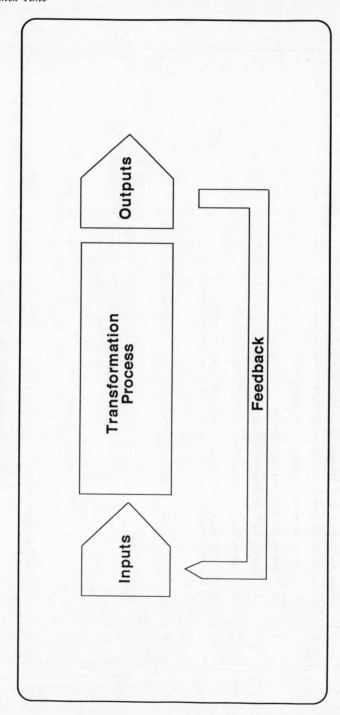

BASIC SYSTEMS MODEL

Inputs

Transformation Process

Outputs

Feedback

PROCESS TRACKING METHODOLOGY

THE OVERALL PROCESS

1. Identify the Starting and Finishing Points of the Process.

2. Identify all the inputs that start the Process in motion.

3. Identify all the Outputs of the Process.

4. Identify the Customer of the Process.

5. Identify Customer Requirements relating to Process Outputs.

6. How do you know if the Process is performing well or correctly?
   (Identify the Feedback elements that help track performance.)

THE "LEVEL ONE" MAP

7. Identify the major phases or steps of the Process.

THE "LEVEL TWO" MAP

8. For each major phase or step of the process, track and record all the Sub-steps of the Process.
   Map what actually happens; not "ideal" procedures. For each Sub-step:
   - Identify Inputs and Outputs.
   - Collect all documents, reports, papers or Information Technology used.
   - Identify all approvals, verifications and feedback that enters or leaves the Sub-step.

9. Build a Process Time-Line

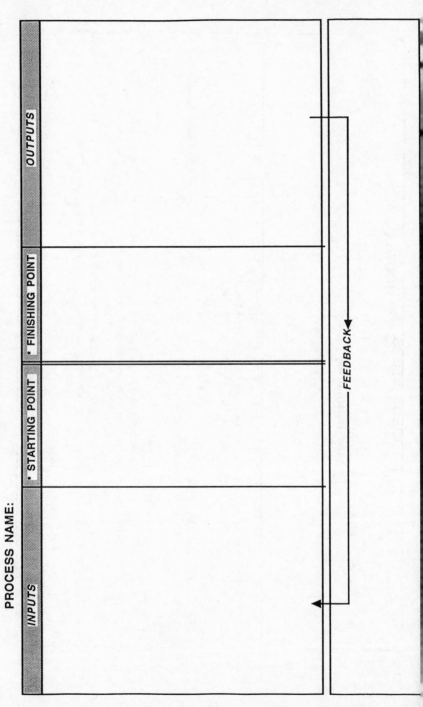

PROCESS STEPS

**Overall
or
per Role/Activity**

Step 1:

169

INTERVIEW QUESTIONS

THE 'LEVEL TWO' MAP

For each major phase or step of the process, track and record all the Sub-steps of the Process. Map what actually happens.

OVERVIEW

1. What is the Purpose of your job or activity?

2. Can you summarise for us your role within the Daily Follow-up Process?

INPUTS

1. What comes to you before you actually begin your work?

2. Who gives it to you? (What is the Source?)

3. In what form and quantity does it come?

4. Do you get what you need on time?

5. Are you dependent on getting all information before you begin?

INTERVIEW QUESTIONS (con't.)

PROCESS

1. What is the first thing you do?

2. What is the last thing you do?

3. What are the main steps you carry out in between?
   What actually happens? Please do not give us "ideal" procedures.
   Please walk me through the specific actions and tasks you perform.

4. Check to see steps are in the right sequence.
   Identify all approvals, verifications and feedback that enters or leaves each Step.

5. Collect all documents, reports, papers or information collected or produced at each Step.

   Identify Information Technology tools and activities.

INTERVIEW QUESTIONS (con't.)

OUTPUTS

1. What type of Outputs do you produce at each Step?

   (Hard copy - Electronic - Verbal - Other)

2. What do you do with them? Where do they go?

3. How do you send them out?

   (By mail - By hand - Electronically - By telephone - Other)

FEEDBACK

1. Do you get any feedback about what you send or produce?

2. How do you know that what you do is:

   - needed / useful?

   - meets customer requirements?

   - meets performance targets?

Step 2:

ROLE or ACTIVITY SUB-STEPS

Inputs
+
Source

Outputs
+
Recipient

INTERVIEW QUESTIONS (con't.)

REVIEW

1. Is this everything that happens? Did we leave anything out?

2. Build a "Process Time-Line". Indicate the dates or times of:

   - The Starting Point
   - The Finishing Point
   - Key Actions (Inputs, Process, Outputs, Feedback)
   - Key Decisions

3. If your boss wanted it done right this minute, is this exactly what you would have to do to get it done immediately?

4. Looking at this Map, what suggestions would you make for improvement?

174

Step 3:

LINKING

Sub-Steps, Roles and Activities

Role/
Activity 1

Role/
Activity 2

Role/
Activity 3

Step 4:

PROCESS TIME-LINE

Indicate date(s) or time(s) of:

- Starting Point
- Key Actions
- Key Decisions
- Finishing Point (if known)

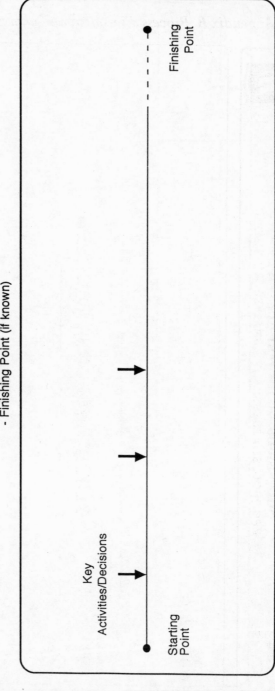

Key
Activities/Decisions

Starting
Point

Finishing
Point

AIR MILES RESTRUCTURING PROJECT
BPC PROCESS ASSESSMENT & ANALYSIS WORKBOOK

CLIENT RESPONSE PROCESS

PROCESS DATA

PROCESS	Client Response Process
PROCESS CUSTOMER	Air Miles' Clients
DEPARTMENTS	Sales, Marketing, Travel Products, Relationship Management, Client Services Unit, Systems Client Delivery
DATE	July, 1994

STARTING POINT OF PROCESS	FINISHING POINT OF PROCESS
Develop strategic, marketing and sales guidelines.	Delivery of contracted services to client.

CURRENT BUSINESS REQUIREMENTS (resources)		CURRENT MANAGEMENT REQUIREMENTS (operational)		CURRENT CUSTOMER REQUIREMENTS (product)	
Time	On-going.	Quality	Resolution of all client and collector complaints.	Format	Appear tailor-made.
Finance	salaries & direct costs for simple and complex sales.	Product	80% standardised products.	Delivery time	As requested.
People	No increase/decrease.	Cycle Time	Establish current cycle time and reduce by 40% within 12 months.	Pricing	Competitive with other forms of promotional activities.
Materials	Project planning software. IT support.	Productivity	X% gross profit margin & quantity of Air Miles sold.	Technical spec.	Meets contractual specifications.

178

PROCESS DATA (Ctd)

SCOPE - OTHER DEPARTMENTS' INVOLVEMENT & ROLES

Air Miles Corporate	Provide corporate strategy and exclusivity guidelines.
British Airways	Contract approval.
Collector Services	Assess impact of potential sales on collector services and supportive sales.
Finance	Assist in determining/evaluating process costs.
Legal	Provision of standard contracts and strategic contracts.
External suppliers	As needed.

ASSUMPTIONS

Air Miles has the in-house capability to run a process-based organisation.

Processes and products can be costed.

Standard products can be built.

Client doesn't insist that sales person is in charge of relationship management.

Project continuity can be maintained during hand-over from sales.

Other Air Miles departments will adhere to the requirements of client's development plan.

External suppliers will deliver as expected.

PERFORMANCE FEEDBACK

Internal	Tracking of Air Miles and other products sold & gross profit margins by product/programme line.
External(customer)	Client satisfaction survey. Sales, Relationship Management and Senior Management visits.

PROCESS ASSESSMENT

PLUS	MINUS	INTERESTING
• A process-based organisation which provides a platform for continuous improvement.	• Feedback loops still to be implemented.	• How Air Miles adapts to the change from a functional organisation to a process one.
• 85% of the processes already exist.	• Processes still to be costed.	• If staff capabilities match challenges posed by changes.
• Costed processes allow targets to include gross profit margins and gross sales.	• Need for further process education within Air Miles.	
• Costed development plan enables strategic decisions on unprofitable contracts to be taken.	• Process quality gates need to be established.	
• Resource requirements for strategic sales known earlier - better commitment of company resources.	• Not all processes implemented. (approx. 15%)	
• Market differentiation maintained at lower costs due to menu of standardised products which reduces amount of customisation.	• Human resource allocation not completed.	
• Early client validation process will reduce cost of failed sales.		
• A more directed sales force (aiming for targets and adhering to margins).		
• Interfaces/responsibilities/roles between sales and relationship management clearly defined- better accountability and performance.		
• Interfaces/responsibilities/roles between collector response process and client response process clearly defined - better accountability and performance.		

ACTION REQUIRED

CONTINUE	STOP	START
• To build standard product packages.	• Using sales people as relationship managers.	• Documenting performance.
• To focus on client/collector requirements.	• Selling unnecessarily tailored packages.	• Building-in process quality gates.
• Product/service costing.	• Selling non-profitable/non-strategic services.	• Using standard contracts for all simple sales.
		• Preparing a financial reporting system.
		• Process costing.
		• Using process maps as catalyst for change.
		• Putting cycle times on processes.
		• Implementing Reengineering decisions.

Index